LAW OF TRANSFER OF PROPERTY

POOJA AGARWAL

Contents

PREFACE

POOJA AGARWAL

As the mind having dynamic perception the author having keen interest in writing and having proficiency in such field that causes the birth of this book. A transfer refers to a conversion of a thing from one person to another person. Property may be defined as anything physical or a virtual entity owned by an individual or a group of people. A property can be transferred from one person to another person by transferring rights, or interest, or ownership, or possession the party can satisfy either or all the ingredients. Basic objective of this act is to formulate rules, regulations and procedures for transfer of property. The Transfer of Property Act 1882 is an Indian legislation which regulates the transfer of property in India. It contains specific provisions regarding what constitutes a transfer and the conditions attached to it.

I

PRELIMINARY

INTRODUCTION

By its very existence, society mandates interaction, exchange or transfer. A property, movable or immovable, is transferred from one person to another under various situations and circumstances and for different values. The transfer may be a gift, an inheritance or an asset acquired by paying full value. Also, there are different laws/legislations governing the transfer of property, movable and immovable under different circumstances.

When a movable property is transferred inter-vivos (i.e. between two living persons), Sales of Goods Act, 1930 comes into play. When an immovable property is transferred from living person to living person(s), the Transfer of Property Act, 1882 comes into play. In case, the property is transferred from a dead person to a living person(s) i.e. by operation of law, the law applied will be the Law of succession. Should a person die without leaving a will (intestate), the law of intestate succession is applicable and in cases where a person dies leaving a will, the law of testamentary succession is applicable.

Transfer of property Act, 1882 is one of the most important branches of the law of property. It was enacted in the year 1882 and contains 137 sections and is divided into 8 chapters. The Act came into force with effect from 1st July, 1882. It mainly deals with the transfer of immovable property and also movable property between two living persons i.e. transfer inter vivos. The Act does not apply to transfer by operation of law (E.g.: Succession, Court Sales, insolvency etc.)

SCHEME OF ACT

The Transfer of Property Act mainly deals with the transfer of immovable property. As stated above, some of the Sections also deal with movable property.

- **Sections 5 to 37** of Chapter-II are applicable where the property is immovable or movable,
- Chapters III to V containing **Sections 54 to 117** deal with immovable properties only.
- Chapters VI to VIII containing **Sections 118 to 137** are applicable to both immovable and movable properties.

BACKGROUND

In India, the personal laws governed the transfer of property assisted by orders of Courts under Civil Procedure Code before the Transfer of Property Act, 1882 came into existence. Transfer of movable goods was regulated to an extent by the Indian Contract Act, 1872. For transfer of immovable property, the Anglo-Indian courts often resorted to principles of Justice, Equity and Good Conscience as it prevailed in England at the time. This rarely helped owing to the vast differences in customs and society of the two countries. Of course the rapidly growing commerce and infrastructure in the late nineteenth century lead to more conflicts even in business. Thus, an immediate need was felt for a clear and pragmatic law regarding property and transfers suited to India and its peculiar problems as well as to take care of the potential economic problems. The task of drafting such legislation fell upon the First Law Commission and was later referred to the Second Law Commission. A Bill, finally presented to the Legislative Council, became a law on the 17th of February 1882 and came into force from 1st July of the same year.

OBJECTIVES

The Transfer of Property Act, 1882 (hereinafter referred to as the 'TP Act, 1882') was intended to define and amend the existing laws and not to introduce any new principle. It applies only to voluntary transfers. The following may be enumerated as the objectives of the Act:

a. As per the preamble of the Act, the TP Act, 1882 is to amend or regulate the law relating to transfer of property by the acts of the parties.
b. The Act provides a clear, systematic and uniform law for the transfer of immovable property.

c. The Act completes the Code of Contract since it is an enacted law for transfers that take place in furtherance of a contract.

d. With provision for inter-vivos transfers, the TP Act, 1882 provides a law parallel to the existing laws of testamentary and intestate transfers.

e. The Act is not exhaustive and provides scope to apply the principles of Justice, Equity and Good Conscience if a particular case is not governed by any provision of law.

SCOPE

Since the T P Act, 1882 is not a complete code of transfer of property; we can say its scope is limited. The Act does not apply to all the transfers taking place in India.

a. *Limitation on Transfer*: The Act applies to transfer by the act of parties and not by application of law. Thus, its operations are limited to transfers by act of parties only except in a few cases saved by Section 2 of the Act.

b. *Not Exhaustive*: There are various kinds of property and various modes of transfer of property. The Act does not incorporate rules for all modes of transfer in existence. The Act does not even claim to be a complete code as apparent from omission of the term 'consolidate' from its Preamble.

c. *Transfer of Immovable Property:* The Act mainly deals with transfer of immovable properties only.

d. *Exemption of Muslim Law:* In case of a conflict between the TP Act, 1882 and rules of Muslim Law, the latter will prevail. Section 2 of the Act does not affect inconsistent rules of Muslim Law. Thus, a settlement made in perpetuity for the benefit of descendants of the settler is a valid wakf (charitable gift) wherein there is an ultimate gift in favour of a charity.

e. *Exemption of Rights and Incidents*: Certain incidents of a contract or the essential nature of property are exemption from the operation of the Act by Section 2. The Act also saves certain property rights. For example, the right to partition of immovable property is an incident of property but this right is not affected by the provisions of the TP Act, 1882.

TERRITORIAL LIMITATION

A territorial law is a lex loci i.e. law of a particular place and applies to all persons inhabiting the territory irrespective of their personal status. It is different from personal law that generally follows the person. The TP Act, 1882 is a territorial law and its operation extends to the whole of

India except for Punjab. It was not enforced throughout the country in one go. It was made applicable to different parts of the country on different occasions. When the Act was first enforced (1ˢᵗ July 1882), it extended to the whole of 'British India' except Bombay and Punjab. The Act was extended to the territories of Bombay from 1ˢᵗ January 1893. In Punjab, the transfer of immovable property by the act of parties is governed by the rules of Justice, Equity and Good Conscience.

Transfer of property is a 'Concurrent Subject' (Entry 6 of List III (Concurrent List) of Seventh Schedule to Constitution). Both Central and State Government can take legislative action in respect of transfer of property except that relating to agricultural land which is a state subject.

II

IMMOVABLE PROPERTY

Transfer of Property Act primarily governs the transfer of immovable properties. Movable properties are governed by Sale of Goods Act, 1930. Hence, there is a need to understand what is movable and what is immovable property and the ways to distinguish them. The word "Property" has not been defined in TP Act when we examine the Act, we realise that the word has been used in the most widest and generic sense. Property denotes every kind of interest or right that has an economic content.

Property broadly classified into–

1. Movable property
2. Immovable property

The Term "Immovable Property" occurs in various Central Acts. However none of those Acts conclusively define this term. The most important act which deals with immovable property is the Transfer of Property Act (T.P.Act). Even in the TP Act this term is defined in exclusive terminology. TP Act does not actually define immovable property. The definition fails to indicate as to what is "included" as immovable property.

- According to **Section 3 Para 2** of TP Act,

"Immovable Property" does not include standing timber, growing crops or grass. Thus, the term is defined in the Act by excluding certain things. The expression 'standing timber' means trees fit for use for building and repairing houses. Growing crops includes all vegetable growths, which have no existence apart from their produce such as pan leaves, sugarcane etc. Similarly, grass can only be used as fodder and is a movable property.

- As per **Section 3(26)** of the General Clauses Act 1897,

"immovable property" "shall include land, benefits to arise out of land and things attached to the earth, or permanently fastened to anything attached to the earth". This definition of immovable property has reference only to the physical objects and does not furnish an exhaustive test of what is, and what is not, immovable property; The term immovable property includes three tings namely-

- Land;
- Benefits arising out of land; and
- Things attached to earth.

Here, land does not include only the upper surface of the earth but is extensive enough to cover things below it, for instance minerals, wells, tube-wells, rivers, ponds etc. Further, benefits arising out of land means other ancillary rights well connected to land such as right to receive future rent, revenue form agriculture, right to collect lac, leaves or other things from forest trees etc.

- **Section 2(6)** of The Registration Act, 1908 defines "Immovable Property" as under:

"Immovable Property includes land, building, hereditary allowances, rights to ways, lights, ferries, fisheries or any other benefit to arise out of land, and things attached to the earth or permanently fastened to anything which is attached to the earth but not standing timber, growing crops nor grass".
The definition of the term "Immovable Property" under the Registration Act, 1908 is comprehensive. The above definition implies that building is included in the definition of immovable property.
Thus,in essence land included–

1. Earth's surface
2. Earth's surface covered by water
3. column of space above the surface: Objects placed by human agency with the intention of permanent annexation (Eg: buildings, fences, walls)
4. Ground beneath the surface: In its natural state (Eg: Minerals)

Relevant Cases:

- **Ananda Behara v. State of Orissa (AIR 1956 SC 17)** – Right to catch fish from Chilka lake over a number of years, was held to be an equivalent of a benefit to arise out of land
- **Shanta Bai v. State of Bombay (AIR 1959 SC 532)** – Right to enter land, cut and carry away wood over a period of twelve years was held to be immovable property. The right to collect lac from trees is also immovable property.

In this case, it was held that, the intention is important determining a tree whether it is movable or immovable. If the intention is use the tree for the purpose of enjoying fruits, then it will be regarded as immovable property. If the intention is to cut the trees and use it for industrial purpose or wood purpose, then it will be regarded as timber and timber is movable property according to Section 3 of transfer of property act.

"attached to earth" means-

a. rooted in the earth, as in the case of trees and shrubs (subject to the exception of standing timber, growing crops and grass);
b. imbedded in the earth, as in the case of walls or buildings; or
c. attached to what is so embedded for the permanent beneficial enjoyment of that to which it is attached (eg: doors, windows, ceiling fans etc. But ornamental and decorative fittings festivities, electric appliances are not considered in this definition since these are not permanent but only transitory and occasional and secondly they are not in any sense beneficial to the wall or doors. Therefore, these are not immovable property)

TEST

How to determine whether any movable property attached to the earth has become immovable property?

There are two well established tests in English law–

- **Degree/ Mode of Annexation:**

This was the rule laid down in Holland v. Hoggson. If the movable property is resting on the land merely on its own weight, the presumption is that it is movable property, unless contrary is proved. Eg- A brick resting on the land. If it is fixed to the land even slightly or it is caused to go deeper in the earth by external agency, then it is deemed to the immovable property, unless contrary is proved. Eg- A machine fixed to the land by using screws (like in industries)

- **Object/Purpose of Annexation:**

Whether the purpose was to enjoy the chattel (movable property)? Some crushed stones are deposited on a land, so that it can be transported elsewhere in a few days. Here, the intention/object is not to keep the stones permanently. They are to be enjoyed independently of the land on which they are deposited. Or to permanently benefit the immovable property? Some blocks of stones are placed one above the other without using cement, but in a manner that it stays strong and acts as a wall and prevents cattles entering the land. Here, the intention is to make a wall out of the stones. It becomes a part of the property. It benefits the property by protecting to the property.

The difference between movable and immovable property

The following are the differences between movable and immovable property:

- The movable property can be easily transferred from one place to another without changing its capacity or quantity. While an immovable property cannot be easily transferred from one place to the other place and if transferred then it loses its originality and changes in its shape or capacity or quantity.
- The movable property is the property that is not attached to the earth and can be moved. Example- car, books, etc. but if mango trees are cut and sold for timber then it is considered as movable property. In the

case of immovable property, which is attached to the earth and cannot be moved. Example: buildings, trees, etc but if mango trees are sold for nourishment purposes and fruits then it is considered immovable property.

- The registration of the movable property is not mandatory and optional under the Indian Registration Act, 1908. In the case of immovable property, if there is a transformation at any point of time whose subject value exceeds Rs. 100, the registration is mandatory under the Indian Registration Act, 1908.
- The movable property is liable to sales tax, central tax though subject to certain restrictions under the Andhra Pradesh General Sales Tax, 1957 and also the Central Sales Tax. whereas the immovable property is not liable to sales tax but stamp duty and registration fees have to be paid under the respective acts.
- In the case of movable property, the transfer is complete when there is mere delivery with intention to transfer. It is not the same in case of immovable property. In this, the mere delivery with intention does not constitute a valid transfer. The property transferred must be registered in the name of the transferee.

III

ATTESTED

As defined under **Sec. 3** of TP Act,

[attested", in relation to an instrument, means and shall be deemed always to have meant attested by two or more witnesses each of whom has seen the executant sign or affix his mark to the instrument, or has seen some other person sign the instrument in the presence and by the direction of the executant, or has received from the executant a personal acknowledgement of his signature or mark, or of the signature of such other person, and each of whom has signed the instrument in the presence of the executant; but it shall not be necessary that more than one of such witnesses shall have been present at the same time, and no particular form of attestation shall be necessary;]

The expression "attestation" means "to sign and witness the fact of execution of a document by the executants." "Attest" means to testify a fact, to bear witness to a fact. Attestation in relation to a document signifies the fact of authentication of the signature of the executants of that document by the attestator by putting down his own signature on the document in testimony of the fact of its execution.

To understand it better you need to know the term **'Animo Attestandi'**. Animo attestandi means intention of attestation. It says, whoever is attesting witness, his intention should be in attestation.

Concept of Attested

Whenever a document is attested before that an execution happens. Suppose there are two parties and the parties signed that means they did the execution part. Here the parties will be called executant. The person witnesses the process and signed the document is called attesting witness and the whole process is called attestation. The final document is considered as attested.

Object of Attestation

The main object of attestation is to prove the authenticity and truthfulness of the execution. The main purpose of attestation is that there must be free consent i.e. there mustn't be any force, fraud or undue influence.

Essentials of Attested

1. Must have signed
2. The attestation by two or more persons
3. The sign must have been done in the presence of the executant.

Who can attest?

- It's very important to see whether a party has competency or not in attestation.
- A party can't be an attester
- Interested party can't be an attester
- Signing on behalf of an illiterate person is not attester
- If illiterate made mark by himself and the description is written by the scriber, then he is competent attesting witness. A scriber is the person who copies documents.
- Signature of the executant can be attested by an illiterate.
- A person with 'Power of attorney' can't be an attestor as he is interested party.

Case Laws

Here are some of the famous case laws regarding Attested or Attestation.

1.ML Abdul Jabbar Sahib V Venkata Shastri

In this case, court held that if attesting witness has no intention or knowledge then the attestation won't be considered as valid. It will be void. Animo Attentandi is important in attestation.

2.Kumar Harish Chandra Das V Bansidhar Mohanty

In this case, a moneylender gave some money to mortgagee and he gave the money to mortgagor. Here, moneylender was attesting witness and he became an interested party.

Here supreme court held that, interested party can also be an attesting witness. But in general, an interested party can't be an attester. This is an exception.

3.Kundan Lal V Musrafa Rafi

In this case, Musrafa Rafi was the attester and she told that she couldn't see the executant because of she was wearing Burkha. However, court held that, she could have seen if she had an intention.

IV
NOTICE

The last paragraph of the Sec 3 states under what circumstances a person is said to have notice of a fact. Notice literally means knowledge as to existence of certain facts.

Classification of Notice

There are two types of notice under the Transfer of Property Act, 1882 namely, Express or Actual Notice and Constructive Notice. To understand the concept of notice we need to elaborately discuss these two types of notice.

Express or Actual Notice

When a person receives the actual knowledge of a fact or a definite information regarding a legal dispute, it is called actual or express notice. Vague rumor and hearsay are not regarded as an actual notice.

What are the essential conditions for an actual notice?

The following are the essential conditions to constitute an actual or express notice:

1. There must be a definite and direct information or actual knowledge of a fact.
2. A person pertaining to the transaction can only have an actual knowledge.
3. The actual knowledge must be linked with the transaction.

Illustration:

X sells his land to Y. X and Y have a contract. Y gives X 50% of the money and contracted to give the rest after registration of the instrument. Now,

X again sells the same land to Z. If Z knows about the previous contract between X and Y, then Y can go against Z in the court.

Constructive notice

Constructive notice is the knowledge of those particulars facts which a court ascribes on a party. The legal presumption regarding constructive notice is that a person should have known a fact as if he actually knows it. If the situations indicate that a man of ordinary prudence ought to have known a precise fact pertaining to the transaction of transfer then that person will be deemed to know it. This notice works like a provision of law.

In the famous case of **Plumb V Fluitt [1791]** it was upheld by the court that 'Constructive notice is itself an evidence of notice.' The court will not allow any person to disprove it.

What are the essential conditions for constructive notice?

In respect of registered transaction, the followings are the essential conditions for constructive notice:

1. The instrument has to be registered in consonance with the Registration Act, 1908.
2. The instrument has to be duly entered or filed in books kept under section 51 of the Registration Act, 1908.
3. The particulars pertaining to the transaction to which the instrument relates have to be correctly entered in the indexes kept under section 55 of the Registration Act, 1908.

Legal Presumption of Constructive Notice:

In the following circumstances the legal presumption of constructive notice arises –

1. Willful abstention from an inquiry or search
2. Gross negligence
3. Document compulsorily registrable
4. Actual possession
5. Notice to an agent

1. Willful abstention from an inquiry or search

A person has notice if it was his responsibility to make an enquiry of if there was something to put him on an enquiry which if he pursued he would have learnt the truth. The words 'will abstention from an inquiry or search' in section 3 means an abstention from inquiry or search as would show want of bonafides and a mere omission to make inquiries cannot be regarded as sufficient to constitute constructive notice within the meaning of the section.

Illustration: A sells property to B. A got the property by partition and presumption right was reserved in the partition deed. It is B's duty to check the partition deed before purchasing the property, if he abstains himself from enquiring about the partition deed to avoid competition then it is a willful abstention.

2. Gross Negligence

Gross negligence does not mean mere carelessness, it is a degree of negligence so gross in nature that a court of law may treat it as a proof of fraud. If there exists mental indifference to obvious risks then it is a gross carelessness or negligence. What would be gross negligence in one case would not be so in another. It all depends on the man's knowledge and the means of information which lay to his hand.

The main difference between willful abstention and gross negligence is that in latter the intention is not wrong or fraudulent.

Illustration: X purchases a property within the municipality. X did not check whether any municipal taxes pertaining to the property were in arrears. As X failed to check before purchasing it amount to gross negligence.

3. Registration as notice

Registration is considered as constructive notice when the document is compulsorily registrable. The amending act of 1929 made it clear that registration of an instrument relating to immovable property amounts to notice of the instrument from the date of registration.

Registration is notice only in the following circumstances:

- When the instrument is required by law to be registered;
- Registration is notice to a subsequent transferee. Prior transferee is not affected by notice of subsequent transactions from the registration of the same;
- The instrument must have been registered in the manner prescribed by the Registration Act, 1908.

4. Possession as notice

If someone possesses an immovable property, then the purchaser must know that someone is exercising right to possession and enjoyment on that property. In other words, the person dealing with any immovable property shall be deemed to have notice of the title of any person who, temporarily is in actual possession thereof. The possession must be actual.

Illustration: A sells his property to B and then A requested B to let him live in the property as long as A finds a new place to live. Registration was not done. A sells the same property to C. As B's possession is not actual so it is not a constructive notice to C.

5. Notice to agent

The general principle is that a person has notice of fact when information of the fact is given to or obtained by his agent. The knowledge of the agent is regared the knowledge of the principal. This general principle has certain limitations.

Notice to agent is notice to principal in the following circumstances:

- The agent must have actual knowledge of a fact.
- The agent must have obtained the knowledge during agency.
- The agent must have appointed for particular transaction or business.
- The knowledge of fact must be material to that particular transaction or business.
- The agent must obtain the knowledge in a good faith as a reasonable prudent man.

Exceptions to the principle:

- If the agent fraudulently conceals a knowledge of fact with wrongful intention then his knowledge will not amount to principal's knowledge.
- If there is a third party who is involved with agent in the fraud and the third party knows that agent conceals the fact with a wrongful intention then agent's knowledge will not amount to principal's knowledge.

Case Reference
Suleman Khan v Punjab Province [1953] PLR 919
The onus of proving want of notice is on the transferee.
Nagendra Chandra v Parameswar Ray 9 DLR 476
Notice of registration of sale-deed is recognized as constructive notice. This presumption can be rebutted by producing proof that there was no

such notice.

Daniels v Davison [1919] 46 IA 250

Where land is in the occupation of someone other than vendor, the fact of the occupation gives the purchaser constructive notice of any rights of the occupying tenant.

Ranjital v Municipal Board of Lucknow [1936] 12 Luck. 353

A person purchasing property within the municipal limits was bound to inquire whether any municipal taxes in respect of the property are in arrears. If he did not care to do so, it would amount to gross negligence.

Rai Chand v Dattatraya [1964] AIR Bom. 1 (DB)

In some cases, by legal fiction constructive notice may be imputed to the party but in the present case the particulars relating to transaction have not been correctly entered in the indexes kept under section 55 of the TPA, 1882, which is one of the essential conditions of constructive notice so, it cannot be imputed to the plaintiff.

V

ACTIONABLE CLAIM

As the expression **"Actionable Claim"** itself denotes, it is a claim on which action lies for certain reliefs in the law courts. It excludes the claims which have been already adjudicated or decreed so that no further action can be based thereon and also the claims, though actionable are secured by mortgage or pledge or hypothecation. This exclusion is reflected in the definition of "Actionable Claim" contained in Section 3 of the Transfer of Property Act, 1882.

According to section 3 of the Transfer of Property Act, *the actionable claim is a claim to any debt which is not secured by a mortgage, pledge, and hypothecation.*

Essentially, an actionable claim is a claim to any debt or to any beneficial interest in movable property. Under the TP Act, an actionable claim excludes the claims to such debts as are secured by mortgage, hypothecation or pledge of immovable or movable and the claims to any beneficial interest in any movable property that is in the actual or constructive possession of the claimants.

ILLUSTRATION : X is a person who needs a loan or money from Y. Then X takes loan 50,000/- from Y. And Y does not take any security. It means X takes loan 50,000/- from Y without any security. So the debt or claim given by Y is an actionable claim. And if the X failure on his part or not repay the money then Y can approach the Court.

Examples of actionable claims-

· The benefit of a contract giving an option to purchase the land;
· Claim for arrears of rent;

- Claim for rent to fall due in future;
- The benefit of executory contract for the purchase of goods;
- An option to repurchase the properties sold;
- An endorsement on the back of a contract for the purchase of goods by the purchaser that he had sold all his rights and interest in the contract to a person named;

Examples of claims that are not actionable claims-

- A claim which is decreed;
- The right to sue for accounts and to recover money which might be found due on taking accounts from an agent;
- A claim for main profits;
- Relinquishment of interest of a retiring member of joint hindu family business in favour of the continuing co-parcener/s;
- A mere right to sue

Sec. 130: Transfer of actionable claim

The transfer of an actionable claim whether with or without consideration shall be effected only by the execution of an instrument in writing signed by the transferor or his duly authorized agent, shall be complete and effectual upon the execution of such instruments.

The transferee of an actionable claim may, upon the execution of such instrument of transfer as aforesaid, sue or institute proceedings for the same in his own name without obtaining the transferor's consent to such suit or proceeding and without making him a party thereto.

According to Section 130,

· The transfer can be done by only a written instrument;

· And signed by the transferor or his legal agent; and

· The transfer will be complete.

Exceptions of the Sec 130 -Sec 130 does not apply on the transfer of marine and insurance of fire policy.

Under Section 132 of the Transfer of Property Act, defines the liability of the transferee of actionable claim. The liabilities and equities of the transferor are transferred to the transferee.

Case References:

Simon Thomas vs. State Bank of Travancore

In this case, there should be an intention to transfer the debt represented by the written receipts.

Jugalkishore Saraf v. Raw Cotton Co. Ltd

The Supreme Court held that a judgment debt or decree is not an actionable claim for action is necessary.

Lachmi Koeri v. the State of Bihar

The Court has been pointed out the transfer of arrears of rent is a type of a transfer of actionable claim. And the transfer of arrears of rent could be transferred in accordance with the provisions of the Transfer of Property Act.

Rekhath Koeri Case,

The Court said that the transfer of arrears of rent is really a transfer of actionable claim and it could be transferred in accordance with the rules and regulations of Transfer of Property Act.

VI
TRANSFER OF PROPERTY

According to **Section5** of the Act, '**Transfer of Property**' means an act by which a living person conveys property, in present or future, to one or more living persons, or to himself or to himself and one or more other living persons. The property may be movable or immovable, present or future and the transfer can be made orally, unless transfer in writing is specifically required under any law. Any person competent to contract and entitled to transferable property, or authorized to dispose of transferable property on his own, can transfer such property whether in part or whole, absolutely or conditionally.

ESSENTIAL OF VALID TRANSFER OF PROPERTY
Following are eight essential for the valid transfer of property:

1. The transfer must be between two or more living persons. So the transferor and transferee can not be exactly identical.
2. The property transferred must be transferable.It must not what mention in section 6.
3. The transfer must not be -

   ◦ opposed to the nature of the interest affected thereby, or
   ◦ for an unlawful object or consideration, or
   ◦ to a person legally disqualified to be a transferee.

4. The transferor must be according to Section 7-

   - competent to tranafer ,
   - entitled to the transferable property and
   - authorised to dispose of transferable property which is not his own.

5. Under Section 9, the transfer must be made in the mode prescribed by the Act. All necessary formalities like attestation, registration etc. must be complied with.
6. According to Section 13, if, on a transfer, an interest is created in favour of an unborn person, subject to a prior interest created by the same transfer, it must exhaust the whole of the remaining interest of the transferor.
7. Under Section 14 the transfer must not offend the rule against perpetuity.
8. According to Section 25, when the transfer is conditional, the condition must be not be illegal, impossible, immoral or opposed to the public policy.

VII
WHAT PROPERTY MAY BE TRANSFERRED & WHAT PROPERTY CANNOT BE TRANSFERRED

Section6 of the Transfer of property Act lays down that property of any kind may be transferred except as provided under Law for the time being in force. The words 'property of any kind' indicates that transferability is the general rule and the right to property includes the right to transfer the property to another person.

Property of any kind excludes from its purview the future property. A transfer of future property can only operate as a contract, which may be specifically performed when the property comes into existence. **Section6 Clause (a) to (i)** of the TP Act lay down the provisions relating to what property may be transferred and what property cannot be transferred. It runs as follows:

EXCEPTION to the rule - "Property of any kind may transferred"

a. The chance of an heir-apparent succeeding to an estate, the chance of a relation obtaining a legacy on the death of a kinsman, or any other mere possibility of a like nature, cannot be transferred.

b. A mere right of re-entry for breach of a condition subsequent cannot be transferred to anyone except the owner of the property affected thereby.

c. An easement cannot be transferred apart from the dominant heritage.

d. An interest in property restricted in its enjoyment to the owner personally cannot be transferred by him.

e. A right to future maintenance, in whatsoever manner arising, secured or determined, cannot be transferred.

f. A mere right to sue cannot be transferred.

g. A public office cannot be transferred, nor can the salary of a public officer, whether before or after it has become payable.

h. Stipends allowed to military, naval, air force and civil pensioners of the Government and political pensions cannot be transferred.

a. No transfer can be made in so far as it is opposed to the nature of the interest affected thereby; or for an unlawful object or consideration within the meaning of Section 23 of the Indian Contract Act, 1872, to a person legally disqualified to be transferee.

j. Nothing in this section shall be deemed to authorize a tenant having an untransferable right of occupancy, the farmer of an estate in respect of which default has been made in paying revenue, or the lessee of an estate is under the management of a Court of Ward, to assign his interest as such tenant, farmer or lessee."

What property may be transferred?

Right to property includes the right to transfer property or interest, absolute or limited in the property. Property of any kind may be transferred except those enshrined in Clause (a) to (j) of Section 6 of the Transfer of Property Act and any other law for the time being in force may declare such property as not transferable.

What property cannot be transferred?

Section 6 of the Transfer of Property Act provides for the general rules that all kinds of property is alienable/transferable. However, certain exceptions are provided under Clauses (a) to (i).

Section 6(a) : Spes Succession

This section states that:

The chance of heir-apparent succeeding to an estate cannot be transferred.

The chance of a relation obtaining a legacy on the death of kinsman cannot be transferred.

Any mere possibility of a like nature cannot be transferred.

Example 1 : A is the owner of a property, if he dies his son B will get the property as he is the legal heir and here it can be said that B is the heir-apparent. But this same property cannot be transferred to B during the lifetime of A.

Example 2: Son B dies during the lifetime of his father A, if during the lifetime of his father, he transfers the property without his father's consent then the transfer would be void ab initio and is prohibited by law.

Section 6(b) : Right of re-entry

This clause states that the right to resume the possession of the land which could be given to some other person for a certain period. For example, lease cases. As per this, if there is a mere right of re-right for breach of a condition, it later cannot be transferred to anyone except the owner of the property who is thereby affected.

Example : A grants a lease of land to B for 3 years. At the expiry of 3 years, if he transfers the right of re-right to C then this transfer shall be invalid.

Section 6(c) : Easement

An easement means a right that the owner or the occupier of certain land has in his possession for the beneficial enjoyment of the said land. It can be said that the right to use or restrict the use of the property of some other person. An easement cannot be transferred except the dominant heritage.

Example : M, the owner of the house has the right of way over their adjoining land with N. Hence, M cannot transfer his right without transferring the house.

In the case of **Sital v. Delanney**, the court held that an easement cannot be transferred unless the dominant heritage right is attached to it.

Section 6(d) : Restricted interest

A person cannot transfer anything that is interest restricted in the enjoyment to him. Restricted rights are personal and cannot be transferred and if such transfer happens then it would be void. The following types of interest are not considered transferable, such are:

- Service tenure;
- A right of pre-emption;
- Emoluments;
- Religious office.

Example : The right of the priest to receive the offering. This right is his restricted interest and he cannot transfer this to another person who may be a doctor by profession.

Section 6(dd) : Right to future maintenance

This clause states that the right to future maintenance whatsoever cannot be transferred in any manner. This is because the right is solely a personal benefit given to a person and so he cannot transfer his benefit to someone else.

Example : A woman who receives maintenance from her husband under a decree or award or order.

In the case of **Dhupnath Upadhya v. Ramacharit**, it was held that where the property is given as maintenance, then the person cannot transfer the property during her lifetime. A right of maintenance is a personal right and cannot be taken away.

Section 6(e) : Right to sue

According to this clause, a mere right to sue cannot be transferred. A right to sue cannot be transferred as the transferee acquires no interest in the subject matter of the suit as much as the owner of the property would.

Example : X published defamatory statements against Y and Y filed a suit against X. But Y cannot transfer his right to Z to recover damages for him. If Y transfers his right to Z then this transfer will be held void.

Section 6(f) : Public Office

A public office cannot be transferred and so the salary of the public officer, whether before or after it becomes payable. A public officer is a person who is appointed to discharge his duty towards the public and for doing such an Act he is paid in the form of salary. This salary is a personal benefit to him that cannot be transferred.

Section 6(g) : Pensions

Generally, pensions are the monetary value like a salary, given to a person timely who ceased to be a government employee. This pension is his benefit which he cannot transfer just like his salary.

In **Saundariya Bai v. Union of India**, it was held by the court that pension is not transferable and as long as such is in the hands of the government.

Section 6(h) : Nature of interest

According to this section, the Transfer should not affect the nature of the interest of anyone. For example, the public or religious uses or services cannot be transferred. If any transfer whose object is unlawful or has unlawful consideration is not permissible under this section. Also if the property is transferred to someone who is disqualified legally to be a transferee then such transfer is not valid.

Example : X, Y, and Z entered into an agreement for the division of gains among them which they acquired by fraud. Hence, this agreement is void as the consideration is unlawful.

Case laws

Sheshammal v. Hasan Khani Rawther

In this case, it was held that an heir who received an advantage for giving up his future right to property, then the heir could not be allowed the benefit of the doctrine of spes succession.

C. Mohammed v. Ananthachari

In this case, the court held that there cannot be an easement by prescription if the person admits that the property belongs to him. The court defined easement as where an owner of the property has the right over the way of the labs for another purpose which is connected with the beneficial use of his own land.

Ananthayya v. Subba Rao

In this case, it was held that if there is an agreement between two persons who are brothers by relation, and one of them agreed to pay a certain amount of money from his income to his brother for his expense as he takes care of him then in such cases the provision of a public officer would not apply.

Sethupati v. Chidambaram

In this case, the court held that in the right to sue, the word merely means that the transferee has no interest in the subject matter than just a bare right to sue.

Palani Goudhan v. Nallapa Goundan

In this case, the court held that if an ex-minor transfers his property without the authority of his guardian who has sold the property during his minority then he transfers his interest on the property, not a mere right to sue.

VIII

PERSONS COMPETENT TO TRANSFER PROPERTY

Section7 of the TP Act lays down as to who are competent to transfer. This section is silent about the persons in favour of whom transfer can be made. Section 7 says that every person –

a. competent to contract under section 11 of the Indian Contract Act and
b. entitled to transferable property, or
c. authorized to dispose of transferable property which is not his own, is competent to transfer such property,either wholly or partly, and
d. either absolutely or conditionally.

According to Section 11 of the Indian Contract Act, 1872, a person is competent to contract if he is –

- of the age of majority,
- of sound mind and
- is not otherwise disqualified from contracting by any law. A person who is competent to contract is competent to transfer a property.

IX

CONDITION RESTRAINING ALIENATION

Transfer of property from one person to another includes the right to own, right to enjoy and the right to dispose/alienate without any restraint or restriction/condition.

During transfer beneficial ownership is passed from one to the other. Power of alienation is a legal incident of property. Ownership can not be thought of without the right to transfer.

So any restriction on such right of alienation is repugnant to and not allowed by the law. If the transferor imposes any condition or clog on the transferee not to transfer further, such condition is called **"Rule Against Alienability"** and is void under **Sec. 10** of TP Act and the transferee can simply deny or ignore such condition.

Simply put, as per Sec. 10, if the condition or limitation absolutely restrains the transferee from alienating his interest in the property, the condition or limitation is void but the transfer remains valid as if there was no condition at all.

For example, A transfers some property to B as a gift but with the condition that while A is alive, B must not transfer the property to any other person. This condition will be held void as it absolutely restrains B from transferring his interest in the property to another person.

Restraint on alienation may be of two types-

- absolute restraint and
- partial restraint.

Absolute Restraints

An absolute restraint is such a restraint which completely takes away the right of the transferee to alienate or dispose of the property. The transferee can now no longer transfer his interest in the property to another person and he has no freedom to do what he wants with the property in his capacity as the owner of the property.

Section 10 stipulates that any condition imposed on the transferee which would amount to an absolute restraint on the right of the transferee to dispose of his interest in the property shall be void. The property must be transferred to the transferee subject to the condition.

In **Rosher v. Rosher (1884) 26 Ch D 801,** A made a gift of a house to B, and gave a condition that if B decides to sell the house during the lifetime of A's wife, she should have the option of purchasing it for Rs 10000, while the market value of the house was set at Rs 10,00,000. This condition was held to be an absolute restraint and was declared void.

In **Kannamal v. Rajeshwari, AIR 2004 NOC 8 (Mad)**, a life estate was to be created in favour of 'M', but the transferor gave an absolute restriction along with the property transfer to M, whilst divesting himself of all his interests in the property. This restraint was held to be void as there was an absolute transfer.

In **Mohd Raza v. Abbas Bandi Bibi,(1932) 59 IA 236**, a condition imposing restriction for a particular time or transfer to a specific person has been held to be void.

Partial Restraints

A partial restraint is a condition which partially takes away the right of the transferee to dispose of his interest in the property. Here, the right is not taken away substantially. Section 10 does not explicitly talk about partial restraints. A condition imposing partial restriction is valid.

In **Mata Prasad v. Nageshwar Sahai (1927) 47 All 484,** there was a dispute regarding succession between nephew and widow. A compromise was formed that the widow had possession of the property while the title for the same was given to the nephew with the condition that he was restricted from alienating the property during the widow's lifetime. It was held that the compromise and the condition were valid and prudent in the present case.

Exceptions to the restraints

Lease

A lease is a transfer of property wherein the lessee only has the right of enjoyment of the property, while the ownership right is still with the lessor. Conditions imposing restrictions are valid in the case of a lease, where the condition is for the benefit of the lessor or those claiming under him.

In **Raja JagatRanvir v. Bagriden, AIR 1973 All 1**, a condition in the lease that the lessee shall not sublet or assign was held to be valid.

Married Woman

When the property is to be transferred to a married woman, who is not a Hindu, Mohammedan or Buddhist, then the condition restricting alienation can be valid.

Repugnant conditions (section 11)

Section 11 of the Transfer of Property Act contains conditions which are inconsistent with the nature of the interest transferred are repugnant conditions. These conditions come with the transfer when the transfer confers to the transferee, absolute interests in the property. Any condition with a transfer of absolute interests in the property will be void.

When a property is transferred absolutely, it must be transferred along with all its legal incidents. In **Manjusha Devi v. Sunil Chandra, AIR 1972 Cal 310**, the parties entered into a sale for a piece of land. In the sale deed, it was mentioned that the buyer could only use the land for setting up a factory for jute textile manufacturing. It was held that this condition was invalid as the absolute interests in the land had been transferred to the buyer and he could use it as he pleased.

An exception to Section 11

If the transferor has another piece of immovable property, he may, for the benefit of that property, impose conditions of restrictions on the transferee's right of enjoyment. For example, A has two properties: X and Y. A sells them to B with the condition that a portion of X, adjoined to Y, shall be kept open for the benefit of Y. This condition will be valid.

Positive and negative conditions

Positive conditions: These are those conditions imposed on the transfer where the transferor imposes a condition on the transferee to do some act. For example, A transfers land to B, on the condition that he shall maintain and keep filling up the well on that plot of land. This condition is positive.

Negative conditions: These are those conditions imposed on the transfer when the transferor imposes a condition on the transferee to not do some act. For example, A transfers land to B, on the condition that he shall leave open a four feet wide space on the land, and would not build anything on it.

Difference between Section 10 and Section 11

Section 10 specifies that in a transfer with condition that absolutely restrains the alienation of the property by the transferee, the condition will be deemed to be void.

Section 11 specifies that in a transfer where absolute rights in the property have also been alienated to the transferee, and where a condition is imposed that the transferee cannot, in spite of having the absolute right in the property, do an act for his enjoyment of the property, such condition will be deemed to be void.

Thus, the differences in these sections are that in Section 10 the condition is deemed void due to absolute restrainment and in Section 11, the condition is deemed void due to the transfer being of absolute nature.

Condition of insolvency(section 12)

Section 12 provides that when the transferee becomes insolvent, and if he has some interest in the property that was transferred to him by the transferor, the transferee still would not lose his interest in the property. Hence, any condition stating that transferee shall lose the interest in the transferred property on insolvency and this interest shall be reverted back to the transferor shall be void.

However, this section does not apply to a condition on a lease for the benefit of the lessor or those claiming benefit under him. However, in Smith v. Gronow (1891) 2 QB 394, if lessee assigns the lease and then is rendered insolvent, then this condition will not apply.

X

TRANSFER FOR THE BENEFIT OF UNBORN PERSON

The Transfer of Property Act, 1882 deals mainly with the transfer of immovable properties between two living persons i.e. transfers inter vivos. According to Sec. 5 of the TP Act, the general rule is that property can be transferred in favor of living person. Therefore, a transfer cannot be made directly in favor of an unborn person. Here, the term "living person" includes juristic person such as company, registered firm etc. Under the English law as well as Indian law a child in mother's womb is considered to be in existence. But a child who is not in mother's womb is not considered to be in existence. But Sec. 13, 14 and 18 of the TP Act deal with the law with respect to the transfers for the benefit of an unborn person.

Section 13 embodied the "**Rule Against Double Possibilities**" what is known in England as the rule in **Whitby** v. **Mitchell**. Section 14 of the Transfer of Property Act controls section 13.

Section 13 lays down that where on a transfer of property, an interest therein is created for the benefit of a person not in existence at the date of the transfer, subject to a prior interest created by the same transfer, the interest created for the benefit of such person shall not take effect, unless it extends to the whole of the remaining interest of the transferor in the property.

Such an interest may be created for the benefit of an unborn person if the following conditions are fulfilled-

1. No direct transfer.
2. Interest of the unborn person must be preceded by a prior interest.
3. The unborn person must come into existence before the prior interest comes to an end i.e. before the death of the last life estate holder and he must have the interest at the latest when he attains majority.

The whole of the remaining interest of the transferor in the property must be comprised in the interest created for the benefit of such unborn person.

Essential Elements of Section 13

The essential elements of section 13 have been discussed below. They are as follows:

1. No Direct Transfer

A transfer cannot be directly made to an unborn person. Such a transfer can only be brought into existence by the mechanism of trusts. It is a cardinal principle of property law that every property will have an owner. Accordingly, if a transfer of property is made to an unborn person, it will lead to a scenario wherein the property will remain without an owner from the date of transfer of property till the date the unborn person comes into existence.

2. Prior Interest

If the circumstances are such that there is no creation of trust, then in that case the estate must in some other person between the date of transfer and the date when the unborn person comes into existence.In simpler words we can say that the interest in favour of an unborn person must always be preceded by a prior interest created in favour of a living person.

3. Absolute Interest

The entire property must be transferred to the unborn person. The transfer to an unborn person must be absolute and there should be no further transfer from him to any other person.An interest which remains only for the lifetime cannot be conferred on an unborn person. Under the English law, an unborn person can be conferred an estate only for his lifetime. This concept of English law, however, is subject to a restriction known as the rule of double possibilities. This rule was recognised in the case of Whitby Mitchell. The rule states that life interest to an unborn person should not be transferred as doing so will give rise to existence of two possibilities. The first possibility will be the birth of the unborn person to whom the life estate was to be transferred and the second possibility will be the coming into existence of issues of that unborn persons. Thus, the transfer of property to an unborn person can be permitted only if the absolute interest is transferred and not just the life estate.

Illustration

"A" owns a property. He transfers it to "B" in trust for him and his intended wife successively for their lives. After the death of the survivor, it is to be transferred to the eldest son of the intended marriage for his life, and after his death, it is to be transferred to A's second son. The interest so created for the benefit of the eldest son does not take effect because it does not extend to the whole of A's remaining interest in the property.

When an Unborn Person Acquires Vested Interest

The provisions of section 20 of the Transfer of Property Act, 1882 mention the concept that in what circumstances unborn person acquires vested interest. Unborn person may not be able to enjoy the possession of property as soon as he is born but he may, however, acquire a vested interest in the property since his birth. Where, on a transfer of immovable property interest is created for the benefit of an unborn person, he acquires upon his birth, a vested interest, although he may not be entitled to the enjoyment thereof immediately on his birth.The mentioned provision however may be waived off if the terms of the agreement mention a contrary clause.

The section lays down that an interest created for the benefit of an unborn person vests in that unborn person as soon as he is born. Such interest remains vested interest even though he may not be entitled to the enjoyment thereof immediately on his birth.

For example, if "A" transfers an estate to trustees for the benefit of A's unborn son with a direction to accumulate the income of such estate for a period of ten years from the date of the birth of A's son and then to hand over the funds to him. A's unborn son acquires a vested interest upon his birth, although he is not entitled to take and enjoy the income of the property for a period of ten years.

Girjesh Dutt vs. Datadia

"A" made a gift of her properties to "B", who was her nephew's daughter. The gift made by A was made for the life of B and then to B's daughter without power of alienation and if there was no heir of B, whether male or female, then to A's nephew. B died without having any children. Thus considering the facts of the case, the court held that the gift in favour of unborn daughters was invalid under Section 13 as the gift was a limited interest and also subject to the prior interest in favour of B.

Raja Bajrang Bahadur Singh v. Thakurdin Bhakhtrey Kuer.

In the instant case the Apex Court had observed that no interest can be created in favour of an unborn person but when the gift is made to a class or series of persons, some of whom are in existence and some are non existent, it does not fail completely, it is valid with respect to the persons who exist at the time of testator's death and is invalid with respect to the rest.

XI

RULE AGAINST PERPETUITY

The dictionary meaning of the word **'perpetuity'** is 'continuing forever'. Here under **Sec. 14** the term "perpetuity" refers to tying up of property for an indefinite period or forever. According to Jarman, perpetuity, in the primary sense of the word, is a disposition which makes property inalienable for an indefinite period. If properties are blocked forever from being alienated, the commerce would be obstructed, capital investment of the country would be withdrawn from trade and every branch of industry would be diminished. Certainly, it would obstruct the national prosperity. There are some persons who wish to retain their properties in their own family from generations to generations perpetually. But, it is the policy of the law to prevent creation of perpetuities.

To protect this situation Sec. 14 of the Transfer of Property Act has embodied the rule against perpetuity. The rule is founded on the general principle that the transfer shall be void which tend to create in perpetuity or place property for ever out of the reach of exercise of the power of alienation.

Transfer to take effect on failure of prior interest – Where, by reason of any of the rules contained in sections 13 & 14, an interest created for the benefit of a person or of a class of persons fails with regards to such person or the whole of such class, any interest created in the same transaction and intended to take effect after or upon failure of such prior interest also fails."

Prior Interest fails under section 13 & 14: Before section 16 comes into operation, the prior interest created should fail. This is because it does not fulfil either of the conditions mentioned in section 13 & 14 for a person or a class of persons.

Fate of second interest: On failure of prior interest, the second interest which too is created in the same transaction, and was to be exercised after or on failure of prior interest, shall fail for all purposes.

Example: A transfers a piece of land to his friend B for life, and afterwards to his friend C for life, then to his friend D for life, and then to the son that may be born to B, for his son's life, then to the son that may be born to C for his life, and then ultimately to the son that may be born to D forever. In case of such disposition of the land, B cannot alienate the property, because he has only a life interest therein. For the same reason, neither C nor D, nor the sons of B and C can alienate the property. When the property finally vests in D's son, only he will be entitled to alienate the property. This would be certainly a restraint on the free alienation of the piece of land for a considerable long period.

Section 14 prevents this and lays down that one can tie up property and as for instance, if a transfer is made by A in favour of B for his life, afterwards in favour of C, D and E, successively for their lives, who are all living persons, the transfer is valid because all the persons benefited are in existence at the date of transfer.

According to the English law, the vesting of property can be postponed for any number of lives in being and an additional term of 21 years afterwards, & for as many months in addition as are equal to the ordinary period of gestation, should gestation exist. **But according to the Indian law,** the vesting can be delayed beyond the lifetime of persons in being for the period only of the minority of some person born in their lifetime.

Object of Rule

To prevent the property from being tied up forever; Betterment in trade and commerce; Betterment of the property. Protecting the interest of owner of the property otherwise he will not be able to dispose of the property even in case of emergency.

Principle Behimd the Rule

The basic principle upon which this rule is made is public policy. In absence of this rule against perpetuity, all the properties in the world would have been static and of no use to he economy as a whole.

Condition Necessary:-

1. There is an alienation of property.

2. The transfer being made is for the benefit of an unborn child giving him absolute interest.

3. The transfer of interest to beneficiary is herald by life or limited interest of living persons.

4. The unborn person in favor of whom the transfer is done must be born before the death of last preceding living person.

5. Conferring of interest to beneficiary may be postponed only to the life of living person plus minority of the beneficiary; not beyond that.

The following are the exceptions to the rule against perpetuity-

1. The rule has no application where land is purchased or property is held by a corporation.
2. This rule is does not apply when the transfer creates only a personal obligation and does not affect the interest in the property.
3. Gifts to charities such as transfer for the benefit of public, for the advancement of religion, knowledge, health, commerce, safety, or any other object beneficial to the mankind do not fall within this rule.
4. A covenant of redemption in a mortgage is not affected by this rule.
5. A covenant for pre-emption in respect of land unrestricted in point of time is not affected by this rule.
6. Where only a charge is created on any property and such a charge does not amount to transfer of any interest, that charge does not fall within this rule.
7. The contract for perpetual renewal of a lease does not come within the purview of this rule.
8. Provision for the payment of the debts of the transferor.

Anand Rao Vinayak Vs Administrator general of Bombay (1896)

Bombay High Court in this case declared that when the gift was made of movable property in favor of son with gift of shares in the property to son's sons son when the attained the age of 21 ,is void.

XII

RULE AGAINST ACCUMULATION OR DIRECTION FOR ACCUMULATION

The term **"accumulation"** literally means *increase of principle by re-investment of interest.* Sec. 11 says that condition which restrains the enjoyment of property which is absolutely transferred is void. A direction for accumulation of income is a particular mode of restraining the enjoyment of property. But, as contrary to Sec. 10, **Sec. 17** provides an exception and permits a direction for accumulation of income to operate in certain cases. The maximum permissible time period upto which income of the property may be accumulated is:

a. Life of the transferor or,
b. A period of 18 years from the date of the transfer, whichever is a longer period.

So a direction of postponement of beneficial enjoyment or in other word which makes accumulation of income beyond this period of maximum permissible limit is void.

Illustration: A transfers his properties to B for life with a direction that the income of the said properties shall be accumulated during A's life and shall be given also to C. The direction for the accumulation of income is valid, upto life of B. A transfer a property to B for life and thereafter to B's such son who first attains the age of 25 years with a direction for accumulation of income till B's first son attains 25 years. The direction of the accumulation of such income is void, reason it is beyond the permissible limit (life or 18 years). A transfers property to B in 1960 with a direction for the accumulation of its benefits upto 1990. A dies in 1985 thus the transferor lives for 25 years which is more than 18 years. The direction for accumulation is valid upto 1985 (for 25 years) because it is the longer period.

Sec.17 is subject to the following 3 exceptions-

1. **Payment of Debts**- The period of accumulation can be exceeded in case of payment of debts. For example– A makes a gift of his house to B with a direction that from the rents of the house B shall pay Rs 500 per months towards the satisfaction of a debt of Rupees 10,000/- incurred by A. The direction of the accumulation of income is valid even it continues after the life of A or expiry of period of 18 years.
2. **Raising Portions**- Portion ordinarily means a part or share which points to the arising of something out of something less for the benefit of some children or class of children
3. **Preservation and maintenance of the property**- For the maintenance of property/preservation of property, it is allowed.

XIII

VESTED AND CONTINGENT INTEREST [Sec. 19-24]

VESTED INTEREST

Vested interest is defined by **Sec. 19** of the TP Act. When a person has fixed right of present or future possession of property he is said to have Vested Interest in the property.

Sec. 19 says that "*where, on a transfer of property, an interest therein is created in favour of a person without specifying the time when it is to take effect, or in terms specifying that it is to take effect forthwith or on the happening of an event which must happen, such interest is vested, unless a contrary intention appears from the terms of the transfer.*"

It is further provided by Sec. 19 that a vested interest is not defeated by the death of the transferee before he obtains possession.

It has been explained by Sec. 19 that an intention that an interest shall not be vested is not to be inferred merely from a provision whereby the enjoyment thereof is postponed, or whereby a prior interest in the same property is given or reserved to some other person, or whereby income arising from the property is directed to be accumulated until the time of enjoyment arrives, or from a provision that if a particular event shall happen the interest shall pass to another person.

The main characteristics of vested interest are as follows-

1. Vested interest does not depend upon the fulfilment of any condition. It creates an immediate and present right though the enjoyment may be postponed to a future date.
2. Vested interest is not defeated by the death of the transferee before obtaining possession. If the transferee dies, his vested interest passes on his heirs.
3. Vested interest is heritable and transferable also.

ILLUSTRATION: if X executes a deed of gift in favour of Z and directs that Z shall not take over possession of the gifted property till the death of X and his wife Y. Here, Z acquires a vested interest in the property but the enjoyment of the property by Z is postponed. And if Z dies before taking over possession of the property, his vested interest will not be defeated but his heirs will inherit to his vested interest.

Lachman v. Baldeo

A person transferred a deed of gift in favour of another person but directed him that he will not get the possession of that property until the transferor himself dies. The transferee will have a vested interest even though his right of enjoyment is postponed.

CONTINGENT INTEREST

Contingent interest is defined by **Sec. 21** of the TP Act.

Sec. 21 provides that "*where, on a transfer of property, an interest therein is created in favour of a person to take effect only on the happening of a specified uncertain event, or if a specified uncertain event shall not happen, such person thereby acquires a contingent interest in the property. Such interest becomes a vested interest, in the former case, on the happening of the event, in the latter, when the happening of the event becomes impossible.*"

But there is one exception. Where, under a transfer of property, a person becomes entitled to an interest therein upon attaining a particular age, and the transferor also gives to him absolutely the income to arise from such interest before he reaches that age, or directs the income or so much thereof as may benecessary to be applied for his benefit, such interest is not contingent.

The following are the main characteristics of a contingent interest-

1. When the transferee dies before obtaining possession, the contingent interest fails, and the property reverts to the transferor.

2. Contingent interest is depended entirely upon the fulfilment of a condition. Therefore, in the event of non-fulfilment of the condition, the contingent interest fails.

3. Contingent interest is transferable. But the question whether it is heritable or not depends on the nature of the contingency.

Leake v. Robinson

The court held that whenever a condition involves a bequest that is to be given 'at' a particular age or 'upon attaining' a particular age or 'after' attaining this particular age, then it can be derived that the transfer involves a contingent interest.

DIFFERENCE BETWEEN THE VESTED AND CONTINGENT INTEREST

As for example of contingent interest, if a sum of money is bequeathed to A, in case he shall attain the age of 18 or when he shall attain the age of 18. A's interest in the legacy is contingent until the condition is fulfilled by his attaining that age.

VESTED INTEREST

1. Vested interest is created without specifying the time when it is to take effect.

2. In case of vested interest, it is to take effect forthwith or on the happening of an event which must happen.

3. Vested interest is not depended upon the fulfilment of any condition. It creates an immediate right in favour of the transferee though the enjoyment of the property by the transferee is postponed.

4. Vested interest is not defeated by death of transferee before he obtains possession. Vested interest is heritable and transferable.

5. In case of a vested interest, if the transferee, in whose favour the interest is created, dies before taking possession of the property the interest passes on his heirs.

6. In case of vested interest a right with respect to the property is created immediately though the enjoyment is postponed.

CONTINGENT INTEREST

1. Contingent interest is created to take effect on the happening of a specified uncertain event.

2. In case of contingent interest, the specified event may or may not happen. If the specified event does not happen, the contingent interest fails.

3. Contingent interest is entirely depended upon the fulfilment of the condition. So, if the condition, which may or may not happen, is not fulfilled, the interest is lost.

4. Contingent interest is also transferable but whether the contingent interest is heritable or not is depended on the nature of the contingency.

5. In case of contingent interest, if the transferee, in whose favour the interest is created dies before obtaining possession, the contingent interest fails and does not pass on his heirs.

6. But in case of contingent interest there is a mere promise to give such right of enjoyment with respect to the property if the condition is fulfilled.

WHEN CONTINGENT INTEREST BECOMES VESTED??

When a property is transferred subject to a condition precedent, i.e. on the happening of a specified uncertain event, the transfer creates a contingent interest in favour of the transferee with respect to the property transferred. When the specified uncertain event happens the contingent interest of the transferee becomes vested interest. In such event, or on the death of the transferee before he obtains possession, the vested interest of the deceased transferee, with respect to the property transferred, passes on his heirs.

XIV
CONDITIONAL TRANSFERS

Sections25to34 of TP Act lay down the provisions relating to conditional transfers. As per Sec. 25, where the interest created on a transfer of property is dependent upon a condition the fulfillment of which is impossible, or is forbidden by law, or is of such a nature that, if permitted, it would defeat the provisions of any law, or is fraudulent, or involves or implies injury to the person or property of another, or the court regards it as immoral or opposed to public policy, such transfer is declared void.

Conditional transfers may take place in two ways-

1. Condition precedent
2. Condition subsequent

CONDITION PRECEDENT

According to **Sec. 26,** '**Condition Precedent**' means where the terms of a transfer of property impose a condition which must be fulfilled before a person can take an interest in the property, that condition is called a condition precedent. The transferee's interest in the property is only contingent until the condition is fulfilled. Sec. 25 to 27 deals with condition precedent. Substantial compliance of a condition precedent is deemed sufficient.

ILLUSTRATION: A transfers Rs. 5,000 to B on condition that he shall marry with the consent of C, D and E. But E dies and B marries with the consent of C and D. B is deemed to have fulfilled the condition. This condition is called a condition precedent.

Dawson v. Oliver-Massey

A is ready to transfer his property to B on the condition that he needs to take the consent of X, Y and Z before marrying. Z dies and afterward, B takes the consent of X and Y so the transfer can take place as there has been substantial compliance.

Wilkinson v. Wilkinson

The condition where one party was required to desert her husband for the transfer to go through, this was held by the court as invalid as it was against public policy.

CONDITION SUBSEQUENT

'**Condition Subsequent**' is defined by **Sec. 28** of the Transfer of Property Act. It is a condition which destroys or divests upon the happening of an event. According to Sec. 28, on a transfer of property, an interest therein may be created to accrue to any person, with the condition superadded that in case a specified uncertain event happens or does not happen, such interest is to pass to another person. Such a condition is called a condition subsequent. A condition subsequent divests an estate from one person and vests it in another person. This may be explained by an example.

ILLUSTRATION : A sum of money is transferred to A, to be paid to him at the age of 18; if he shall die before he attains that age, to B. A takes a vested interest in the transfer subject to be divested and to go to B in case A shall die under 18.

Venkatarama V. Aiyasami Ayar

A prisoner was sentenced for life and before serving his sentence he transferred his property to B with a condition that the interest created in the transferee shall cease to exist if the transferor return from the prison. It was held that the condition imposed was valid therefore when he returned from prison, the transfer in favour of the transferee ceases to exist.

CONDITION PRECEDENT

1. In condition precedent, the estate is not vested in the grantee until the condition is performed/fulfilled.
2. Vesting of estate is postponed till the condition is performed.
3. Once the interest is vested it can never be divested on the ground of non-fulfilment of the condition.
4. Acquisition of an estate is affected in the condition precedent.

5. In case of condition precedent, the transfer is void if the condition is i) impossible in performance, ii) immoral and iii) opposed to the public policy.
6. In condition precedent the condition must be valid in the eye of law.
7. The condition precedent may be subsequently complied with. The doctrine of Cypress applies.

CONDITION SUBSEQUENT

1. A condition subsequent is one by the happening of which an existing estate will be defeated.
2. Vesting is immediately completed and not postponed.
3. Though the interest is vested it is liable to be divested on the ground of non-fulfilment of condition.
4. Retention of the estate is affected in the condition subsequent.
5. In case of condition subsequent, the transfer is valid if the condition is i) impossible of performance, ii) immoral and iii) opposed to the public policy, only the condition will be ignored .
6. In condition subsequent the condition's invalidity will be ignored.
7. The condition subsequent must be strictly complied with. The doctrine of Cypress does not apply.

XV
DOCTRINE OF ELECTION

The principle of the doctrine of election was explained in the leading case of **Cooper v. Cooper. Sec. 35** of the TP Act embodied the doctrine of election. *The doctrine of election is based on the principle of equity.*

Election means the right of choosing between presumptive alternatives. The doctrine of election is applicable to both movable and immovable properties. It states that, when one professes to transfer the property over which he has no right, without having informed the owner, he must approach the owner to seek its disposal. The owner must decide whether or not to allow it. Henceforth, it can be inferred that he has the right to exercise the doctrine of election to either confirm or dissent during a transaction.

ILLUSTRATION : Raj transfers his house to Mr. Rahul, by a gift and in the same gift deed asks Me Rahul to transfer his shop to Anuj. Rahul may elect to accept the transfer or reject the transfer. If Rahul accepts the transfer, he will get the house, but in that case, he will also have to transfer the shop to Anuj.

Understanding the Doctrine of Election

It provided that where a property is transferred to a person, then the transferee can make a choice between whether to accept the transferee or reject it. The burden of the transfer is complimentary along with the benefits of the transfer. In other words, enshrined in legal maxim qui approbat non reprobate i.e Aman cannot approbate and reprobate.

In case the person upon whom a benefit us conferred rejects it, the property which was attempted to be transferred to him will revert to the transferor and it is the transferor who will compensate the disappointed transferee. If the transferor dies, before the transferee makes the election, then the legal heirs of the transferor will compensate the disappointed transferee out if the inherited assets.

The doctrine of election is universally applicable.

In reference to the mode of elections, the election by the owner can either be direct, through communication or indirect, "the acceptance of the benefit by the original owner is subject to conditions:

- He has a duty to elect which he must have the awareness, and
- There must be proof of knowledge of circumstances which would influence the judgment of a reasonable man in making an election.
- Acceptance for two years (Section 188(1) of the Indian Succession Act)
- Status quo cannot be restored

The Necessary ingredients for the Doctrine of Election:

- The person transferring the property should transferor should not be the owner of the property.
- The person transferring must at the same time and in the same instrument, grant some of his own property to the owner of the property.
- Both the transfers must be made in the same transaction i.e Transfer of the property of the owner to the transferee and conferring the benefit on the owner of the property. The doctrine of election is not applicable if the transfers are made by virtue of two separate instruments.
- It is required that the owner has a proprietary interest in the property. A person being a creditor is uncommitted in the election as he merely has a personal right to be paid by the debtor.
- The owner is not put to election who does not receive direct benefit under the transaction, but gets some benefit under it indirectly.
- The question of election does not arise when the benefit is received by a person in a different capacity. For example, a person can accept legacy for an estate, at the same time in his personal competence, he could retain the property.

Codrington v Lindsay

Court states that the doctrine of election is based on the principle of equity. One cannot approbate and reprobate at the same time. In layman's terms, where a person takes some pleasure or advantage under a deed or instrument, he must also bear its burden.

There is difference between English and Indian law regarding the doctrine of election.

1. English law applies the principle of compensation while the Indian law adopts the rule of forfeiture.
2. English law does not specify any time within which election is to be made .Indian law specified one year time within which owner of the property is to elect whether he confirms the transfer or dissents from it .If the owner does not comply with such requisition , he is to be deemed to have elected to confirm the transfer.

EXCEPTION

There is a certain exception regarding this rule that if the transferee does not give his or her express consent or conclusive decision, those are:

1. If the transferee full enjoy the beneficiary clause mention in the transfer or where transferee enjoyed the full benefit, then it will be considered as an acceptance by the transferee.
2. If the transferee after one year did not give any consent regarding the transfer of property than transferee is bound to give his or her reply. If he or she did not do that then it will consider that he give the assent for the transfer.
3. The duty of election will be suspended in disability cases like minority, lunacy. Unless the transfer is made by their guardian.
4. If the transferor at the time of making transfer makes a beneficiary clause and an independent beneficiary clause. So, if the transferee did not give assent for the transaction then also he or she will get the independent beneficiary clause.

XVI
DOCTRINE OF ESTOPPEL

Transfer from an unauthorised person- Feeding the grant of Estoppel

A person who holds no interest and authority over a property cannot transfer it. If he does so, such transfer will be considered made by an unauthorised person. Now when he acquires that property, he cannot deny transferring it the person whom he erroneously or fraudulently told that he would transfer that property to him, as the former will be stopped (prevented) from getting back from his previously made statement and now as he had got that property, he has to transfer it to the person whom he promised to transfer that property.

Section 43 is based on two principles-

1. English Common Law of Estoppel.

2. Principle of Equity which states that when a person promises to fulfil a thing more than his capacity, he must do it when he gets the ability.

No person has a right to transfer a property which is beyond his control and when he has no right he should not agree to transfer any interest out of it. When a transfer of interest in land is made, it is known as creating a grant. When that person has no authority of making such transfer, he should not have created any grant in respect of that property.

Therefore, transfer of property cannot be prevented because of his own previous grant which was created by him due to misrepresentation of his right. His earlier grant will support the estoppel. Feeding the grant by estoppel is an English common law doctrine.

Estoppel is a rule of evidence which prevents a person from denying a statement made by him when the statement is going against him. But in the Transfer of Property Act, it shows the relationship between the transferor (before and after he acquires right to transfer) and the transferee for value without any notice.

The law given in section 43 is also based on the principle of equity. Equity states that if a person had made a promise in the past which is more than his capability, he has to fulfil it in the future when he becomes capable of fulfilling it. This is the best example for maxim- equity regards that as done which ought to be done. When the transferor promises to transfer a property which is not in his authority, he commits an unjust act against the transferee. The moment he acquires authority, equity demands from him to transfer the promised property to the transferee. But, a further conveyance is necessary for complete transfer.

Necessary Conditions of Section 43

1. Transferor should not have an authority– First condition for the application of Section 43 is that a transferor should be an unauthorised person, which means he doesn't have any capacity to make a transfer but still he promises the transferee that he will perform the transfer of a particular immovable property. If an unauthorised person promises to transfer the property, the contract is for the creation of a future interest. When he obtains that authority or interest, he becomes liable for fulfilling his promise of transferring the said property. The section compels him to transfer the property in a legal manner which he had promised to transfer without having authority.

2. Fraudulent or Erroneous Representation- The transferor must fraudulently represent to the transferee that he holds an authority to transfer the immovable property. If there is no fraud representation, this section cannot be applied. Misrepresentation can be both in oral or in written but mere silence or inactivity by the transferor can also be amount to misrepresentation. A false statement can be made by both fraudulent and innocent manner or by mistake. If a transferor misrepresents his age or state of mind, Section 43 cannot be applied.

3. Transfer is for a Consideration- This Section is not applicable on gratuitous transfers. So if a transfer by an unauthorised person is made to a transferee as a gift, the transferee will not get the benefit of this section. Where there is value for transfer, there is the applicability of Section 43.

4. The Transferor must acquire the Authority subsequently- The transferor must obtain the authority of a property in the future or subsequently which he had promised to transfer when he had no authority or interest. The authority acquired may be through transfer inter vivo or by the law. Authority can be transferred through exchange or gift deed or through will or inheritance. But the section will not be applicable to the involuntary transfers like auctions or sale by the order of the Court. An auction purchaser cannot take the benefit of this Section.

5. Discretion of the Transferee- The transfer will not pass automatically to the transferee. The transfer depends upon the discretion of the transferee that if all the conditions are fulfilled then he may compel the transferor to transfer the title in his favour. It totally depends upon him whether to enforce his claim or not. This claim cannot be enforced if the unauthorised transferor doesn't get the title by way of exchange, gift, will or inheritance or by any other means during his life time.

If the transferee repudiates his claim then he cannot make it enforceable at the time when the transferor obtains the authority to transfer the property.

Rights of the Second Transferee

The rights of a second transferee have been given as a proviso in the second paragraph of the section. It is for the interest of the bona fide second transferee for value without notice of the 'option' of first transferee. When the second transferee

(1) has a good faith,

(2) paid consideration,

(3) has no notice of the option,

(4) takes the transfer before the option can be exercised, then his claim cannot be affected by the claim of the first transferee under section 43.

If such circumstances arise, the property will be transferred to the second transferee instead of the first transferee.

Illustration- A is a Hindu who has been separated from his father and retains the property x through partition and B his brother gets property Y. A fraudulently represents to C that he has both the properties and sold to him. After sometime, B dies and A becomes the real owner of the property Y also. But before C could exercise his option to compel A to transfer the properties, A secretly sold the property Y to D who purchased it being in good faith and have no idea about the notice of option of C. D has a right to get the Property against the claim of Y. It is important to note that this right can also be used by the subsequent transferee against the claim of second transferee if the conditions mentioned above are satisfied.

Invalid Transfers

The transfer under Section 43 will be invalid if it is forbidden by law, e.g. if the transfer is against public policy or performed by a minor. This section is only to cure the want of title of the transferor at the time of making transfer. If the transfer is void ab initio, the section cannot be applied even if the transferor acquires the property subsequently. Thus if the transferor is a minor at the time when he fraudulently promises to transfer the property, the transferee cannot claim this section even when the minor acquires the property and has also attained the age of majority. Also if the property is non-transferable under section 6, it cannot be validating by applying section 43.

Section 43 does not require that the transferee should take care and act in good faith to check whether his transferor had the authority to transfer. Even if it were so, there is no evident that the transferee knew about the transferor held no interest in the property.

XVII

DOCTRINE OF LIS PENDENS

Section 52 of Transfer of Property Act, 1882 embodies the **doctrine of lis Pendens** (pending litigation) as expressed in the maxim ut lite nihil innoveteur (nothing new should be introduced in a pending litigation).

The doctrine of lis Pendens is of ancient lineage. Originating, it is said in the civil law , it seems to have been operative at an early date as the basis of the common law rule by virtue of which the judgement in a real action was regarded as over reaching any alienation made by the defendant during its pendency. In the course of the time the doctrine was adopted by equity.

Meaning of lis Pendens

lis means an action or suit, 'pendens' is the present participle of pendo meaning continuing or pending, and the doctrine of lis Pendens may be defined as the jurisdiction, power, or control that courts have during pendency of an action over the property involved therein '

Essentials of doctrine of lis Pendens

1) Pendency of suit

According to explanation to Section 52 of Transfer of Property Act, 1882, the pendency of a suit or proceeding begins from the date of presentation of the plaint or institution of the proceedings in a court of competent jurisdiction .A suit instituted in a higher court where it should have been instituted in a lower court is a court having no jurisdiction to try the case (govinda pillai gopala pillai vs aiyyappan krishnan)

The pendency if a suit in foreign court does not create the bar of lis Pendens. Similarly, the doctrine does not apply to property situated outside India (Sivaramkrishna vs K mammu AIR 1957)

2) Bonafide litigation (collusive suits)

The suit or proceeding must not be collusive; it must be a genuine proceeding. A collusive suit is not a real suit but is one in which there is a fraudulent secret understanding between the plaintiff and the defendant that the suit would not be contested with a view to defeat the rights of transferee's of either parties .

3) Right to property must in dispute

The right to an immovable property must be directly and specifically in issue in the suit or proceeding.

4) Transfer by a party to the litigation

The property must be transferred or otherwise dealt with by any of the parties to the suit or proceeding. "parties to the suit " includes the plaintiff and the defendant and / or their demise. Where a legal representative on their demise. Where a legal representative of a defendant in a pending suit effects a transfer and a subsequently substituted in a place of the defendant after his death, lis Pendens will apply (Nallakumara vs pappya

5) Or otherwise dealt with

The property that is the subject matter or otherwise dealt with (eg sale, partition , release, surrender , etc)But that does not include any forcible taking possession.(Dhanisingh vs sushilabhai AIR 1968).

6) Transfer must affect the other party

The doctrine is not applicable where the rights of the transferor alone are affected and not of other party to the suit.(Sripal singh vs naresh)

Exceptions for doctrine of lis Pendens

In spite of the doctrine, however , it is quite open to the court to permit any party to the suit to transfer the property in terms which may think fort to impose. In vinod Seth vs Devinder Bajaj the court permitted the defendant to deal with the property during the pendency if the suit under Section 52 of Transfer of Property Act, 1882. The court observed : "the principles underlying Section 52 of Transfer of Property Act, 1882 is based on justice and equity .

The operation of the bar under Section 52 of Transfer of Property Act, 1882 is subject to such conditions it may impose. That means that the court in which the suit is pending has the power to transfer the property which is the subject matter of the suit without being subjected to the rights of any party to the suit , by imposing such terms as it deems fit.

Having regard to the facts and circumstances, the present case is a fit one where the suit property should be exempted from the operation of Section 52 of Transfer of Property Act, 1882 , subject , to a condition relating to reasonable security, so that the defendant would have the liberty to deal with the property in any manner they may seem fit , inspite of the pendency of the suit .

In **Ayyaswami vs Jayaram Mudaliar AIR 1973 SC 569**, the Court held that the purpose of this provision is not to deprive the parties of every just or fair argument but rather to guarantee that the parties submit themselves to the jurisdiction and authority of the Court which shall determine all claims that are placed before it to the satisfaction of the parties concerned.

In the case of **Hardev Singh v. Gurmail Singh, Civil Appeal No. 6222 of 2000**, the Court ruled that Section 52 of the Transfer of Property Act, would not make void or unlawful any sale of the contested properties, but only puts the purchaser beyond the binding limits of the judgment on the disposition of the conflict.

In the case of **Koyalee v. Rajasthan District, AIR 2009 Raj.28**, the land in question was originally registered in the name of the Plaintiff's husband. After his death, his brother realised and knowing well that the wife of his brother was alive and was the sole legal heir, filed a lawsuit pursuing the Khatedari rights, and pursuant to this, the wife had to contest that she was the sole legal heir of the recorded Khatedar. The brother further went on to transfer the land despite the lawsuit that was pending, since this was done without seeking the Court's permission the transfer was struck down under Section 52 of the Transfer of Property Act as per the Doctrine of lis pendens.

In **Vinod Seth v. Devinder Bajaj, 2010**, though reiterating its power to exclude the suit property from the limitations set out in Section 52 of the Act, it has allowed the Respondent to make a pendente lite move. These exemptions under Section 52 are, however, subject to certain conditions imposed by the Court. In the case at question, the Plaintiff was a contractor who wished to make a profit by constructing a building on the suit-land, and the Defendant wanted to move it to a third party. A total of three lakh rupees was to be deposited as a security by the Defendant to transfer the property in question, The sum the claimant would have profited by. The Court had thus levied the condition for the payment of that sum, which would make the pendente lite transfer legitimate.

The Court's positions on this pendente lite-transfers issue are explained in **Ashok Kumar v. Govindammal and Anr, 2010.** The Supreme Court of India has here reaffirmed that a pendente lite cannot be transferred for a property whose title is the subject of litigation.

XVIII

DOCTRINE OF FRAUDULENT TRANSFER

Section 53 of TPA, 1882 is comprised of two parts. The first part prescribes the principle that, where a transferor transfers his immovable property with the intention to defeat or delay his creditors, that transfer shall be voidable at the option of any creditor so defeated or delayed. Under section 53 of TPA, 1882 the right of a bona fide purchaser will be protected provided that he acted in good faith and he purchases that property for consideration in spite of the fact that the transfer was made by the seller with intent to defeat or delay the creditors.

The second part of **section 53** of TPA, 1882 formulated the principle that, where a transfer of immovable property is made gratuitously or without consideration by the transferor with an intention to defraud the subsequent purchaser, such transfer shall be voidable at the option of such transferee.

The Purpose of Section 53 of TPA, 1882

The main objectives of section 53 of TPA, 1882 are –

- To shield the rights of a bona fide purchaser for value;
- To empower the creditors to avoid any transaction of immovable property made by the debtor/transferor with intent to defeat or delay the creditors;

- To make the assets of the transferor/debtor available to the general body of creditors

Essential Factors Constituting Fraudulent Transfer of Property Under Section 53 of TPA, 1882

1. There should be a valid transfer of immovable property;
2. The transfer should be a fraudulent transfer of property;
3. The transfer should be made with the purpose or intention of defeating or delaying the creditors;
4. The motive to defeat or delay the creditors must exist at the time of transfer made by the transferor.
5. The suit under section 53 must be bought by the creditor in a representative capacity.

Who can sue under section 53 of TPA, 1882?

A fraudulent transfer of property can be set aside by creditors only. The subsequent creditors as well as those creditors existing at the time of fraudulent transfer can sue under section 53 of TPA, 1882.

Who are creditors under the meaning of section 53 of TPA, 1882?

- A landlord is creditor in respect of rents due to him from tenant.
- A Hindu wife with a claim for past-maintenance against her husband is a creditor.
- A Muslim wife to whom dower debt is due is a creditor.
- An auction-purchaser, who is not a decree-holder cannot be a creditor but a decree holder who becomes auction-purchaser of the same property is a creditor.

Nature of the Suit Under section 53 of TPA

A creditor in order to avoid a fraudulent transfer of property must file the suit in a representative capacity. The benefit will be incurred in favor of all the creditors. Order 21, Rule 63 of CPC deals with the rules of representative suit.

Intention to defeat or delay the creditors

The intention and knowledge of the transferor are the gist of this section. Section 53 of TPA, 1882 prohibits transaction which removes property from the debtors for the benefit of the debtor. The debtor's intention must be to benefit himself and to defeat or delay the creditors. Such intention can be proved by circumstantial evidences. From the following factors the court can infer that the transaction is not bona fide –

- Selling all the properties and keeping nothing to himself
- Inadequate Consideration
- Secret Transfer
- Putting all the properties out of the reach of the creditors

Good Faith and Consideration

The purchaser of the property from the transferor must prove firstly, that he had paid a fair and adequate price and secondly, that he was not a party to the fraud. He also has to prove that he acted in good faith. The standards of good faith are –

- There must be an honest dealing between the parties;
- The purpose of the transaction needs to be honest;
- There must exist faithful performance of duties;
- There must be an absence of fraudulent or malice intent.

The term consideration used under section 53 of TPA, 1882 has the same meaning as it has under The Contract Act, 1872. It excludes natural love and affection between the parties.

Defrauding Creditors

The debtor may prefer any creditor he chooses, to discharge the debt. But in doing so, debtor must not retain anything for his own benefit. A mere preference of one creditor to another is not fraudulent under this section. It will not amount to fraud, if debtor wants to shield some property from being proceeded against by creditors while there are other properties from which the dues of the creditors may be realized.

Applicability of Section 53 of TPA, 1882

The section applies in the following cases –

- Hindus and Mohammedans
- Voluntary remissions of debts
- Transfers of movable properties
- Transfer by operation of law
- Partition in joint family

- Surrender of widow's interest by the widow

The Burden of Proof

Under section 53 of TPA, 1882 the burden of proving that a transfer is fraudulent lies on the creditors as he is attacking the debtor with this section. Once the fact is established by the creditor that the transfer was made fraudulently to defeat or delay his claims then the burden shifts on the transferee to prove that he acted in good faith and he is a bona fide purchaser for value and he was not a party to the fraud. So, the transferee can use this section as a shield for his defense and the creditor can use this section as a sword to attack the debtor.

Effects of Section 53 of TPA, 1882

A fraudulent transfer of property is voidable at the option of the creditors and if they not choose to avoid it, the transfer may be valid between the debtor and purchaser. Where a substantial portion of the transfer is fraudulent, the whole transfer shall be treated as fraudulent. Where only a part of the consideration was debt due to the creditor and the rest of it is fictitious the whole transfer must be void.

Exceptions to Section 53 of TPA, 1882

The section will not be applied in respect of following cases –

- Benami Transactions
- Preference of one creditor to over another
- Fictitious transfer of property
- Auction purchases
- Bankruptcy Laws
- Transfer on account of natural love and affection
- Sham Transaction

Karim Dad v Assistant Commissioner 1999 MLD 2371

If the whole transaction is based on fraud and misrepresentation then no valid title can be passed to the transferee by using a forged and fabricated deed.

Musahar Sahu v Lala Hakim Lal 1951 43 Cal. 521

It will not be fraud if the debtor chooses to pay one creditor and leave others unpaid provided that he must not retain any benefit.

Bangladesh v Serajul Haque 11 BLC 714

The defendants obtained an ex parte title decree collusively and by committing fraud. The court after discovering the truth set aside their transfer and declared it fraudulent.

XIX
DOCTRINE OF PART PERFORMANCE

Article 53A of the Act imposes on the transferor a constitutional bar to request the ownership by the transferee of the immovable goods. The transferor shall be disentitled from seeking possession by the proposed transferee.

For example, if the transferor attempts to take over physically, the prospective transferee will be able to institute an action against the transferor to uphold the bar of Article 53A of the Act.

Meaning of Doctrine of Part Performance

The doctrine of contractual part-performance is founded on the general philosophy of fraud prevention. It is intended to secure the transferor who has acquired and invested money to develop it further.

When a transferee has taken custody of the transfer, believing that the transfer is done according to the statute, it would be unfair to encourage the transferee to regard it as an infringer.

Essentials Elements

1. The contract must be of immovable property

- The contract must be for consideration
- The contract must be in writing and signed by him/her or on behalf of him.
- He/she must have some conditions under the contract for a transfer of immovable property.

- The contract or the agreement to sell must be registered.
- The language of the document must be such that the terms are certainly able and not vague must be reasonable and clear if not then the doctrine does not apply.

2. The person to whom it is transferred

- If the property is in custody or some part of it already, or if the property is in possession, the same will occur.
- In the exercise section of the deal, the act of taking possession shall be taken.
- And, to facilitate or invoking the section for the contract, the transferee who was still in charge of the contract has to act something in its advancement.

3. The person to whom the property is transferred is willing to perform the contract or part of it.

4. The person who is transferring the property or any person on behalf of him cannot claim any right on the property on which the person to whom the property is transferred is residing or has possession unless the rights were explicitly mentioned in the terms of the contract.

5. The Doctrine of part performance cannot be invoked if the manner of the contract has not been completed as prescribed by the statute.

- The provision of the section provides:
- This section will not affect the rights of a transferee who did not know the doctrine of part performance of the contract.

Example: If A signs an agreement of sale with B and gives him the possession of the property and B is residing the said property, the later A sells the same property to C through sale deed, and C has no knowledge of the previous agreement then this section will not affect his rights.

Scope of Doctrine of Part Performance

1. In plain reading, a transferor shall take ownership part in the execution of the contract for the property in question, aside from meeting the other provisions, using the shield provided for in this clause, and having done so to promote the contract.

2. Where the relevant contract does not comply with the provisions of a legal contract, the court cannot accept the plea referred to herein. For a transferor to use insurance in this clause, there must then be a legal contract.

3. The purpose of this provision is restricted only to the placing by the transferor, in connection with a property already owned by the transferor, of a bar on the protection of the rights.

4. The section grants no right on unregistered transfer to the transferor to assume custody of the transferor or any other right, it is only applicable to him as a protection.

5. For this clause to apply, the contract must be linked effectively to actions performed in support of the contract or to actions that may be unequivocally alluded to in that contract.

6. Where there is no transfer arrangement or land, the applicability issue of this provision does not arise.

7. The transferor must be the owner to attract the disposition of this section, a sales agreement should be concluded and the transferor's possession should be by that agreement and the transferor has to do something else to support the agreement, and he has to be willing and willing to fulfill his part of the agreement.

The objective of Doctrine of Part Performance

1. The statute obliges both the transferor and the transferee to carry out a transfer. The transferee is generally required to pay the consideration under the terms of the contract and to perform the transfer act in a manner specified by Statute, the transferor is responsible for the transferee.

2. Section 53A centers on maintaining the transferee's right to maintain ownership of the property if the transferee does not have liability because of the fault by the transferor in completing the convey instrument in the way stipulated by statute.

3. This section deals to prohibit the transferor or his successor from using a record that is not being registered provided the transferor performs the contractual portion and has taken care of any immovable property in connection with the conclusion of the contract.

4. To protect his property, the transferor has the right as a defense himself.

5. This section affects partial equality and partial incorporation in the Indian legal framework of the doctrine of partial results.

6. In the absence of a registered agreement, this provision provides for the procedural defense such that a person can retain ownership of his portion of the deal.

7. The primary purpose of this clause is to prohibit the recipient or parties claiming the title in violation of the interests of the other contracting party who has acted as a result of the agreement concluded.

8. This provision provides the accused with the ability to shield his possession from the transferor or others claiming his right under him, such as his heirs, assigned persons and legal agents.

9. This clause stipulates the transferor with a contractual bar that does not confer title to the transferor over the property in question. The transferred party cannot then bring an action to declare his rights to the land and to retrieve ownership on the grounds of the asserted title.

10. The transferee will still exercise his right as a shield, but he will not be allowed to exercise his right as a separate claim, either as complainants or defendant, only because he has satisfied the conditions specified in this clause, he does not assert the right under the present clause.

There is difference in between the English and Indian doctrine of part performance-

A. According to the English law, even oral agreement comes within the purview of this doctrine on the strength of equity but it is not so in India.

B. According to the English law both the plaintiff and defendant can avail of the doctrine whereas it is not so in India. In India this doctrine is used as a shield and not as a sword.

XX

SALE

Meaning of Sale under Transfer of Property Act: – Sale is defined as the transfer of ownership of a property in exchange for a price paid or promised or partly paid or part promised. Sale simply means the purchase and sale of goods and services, the sale of immovable property is provided under Section 54 of Transfer of Property Act 1882.

A sale under transfer of property act is a transfer of ownership for a money consideration. It refers to the complete transfer of all rights in the property sold. No rights in the property sold, are left to the transferor.

Section 54: – Sale ownership is transferred in exchange for a price paid or promised or part-paid and part-promised.

Meaning of Contract for Sale: – A contract for the sale of immovable property is a contract which takes place on the settled terms between the parties. In this, the seller agrees to sell or deliver something to the buyer for a fixed price that the buyer has agreed to pay. A contract of sale of goods is a contract whereby the seller transfers or agrees to transfer the property in goods to the buyer for a price. There may be a contract of sale between one part-owner and another.

What are the elements of Sale?

The elements of Sale are given as follows: –

1. Parties: – In a sale, there must be at least two parties. The person who transfers his property is known as the transferor/seller/vendor and the person to whom the property is transferred is known as the transferee/buyer/vendee.

Seller: –

1. The seller must own the property which he is going to sell.
2. The seller should have legal title to it only then he can sell the property.
3. The seller should be competent to contract.
4. He must not be a minor person.
5. He should not be of unsound mind.
6. He must not be statutorily incompetent.
7. The seller may be a natural person / judicial person, for example, a corporation or any other legal person.

Buyer: –

1. The buyer must be competent to get the ownership of the property.
2. The buyer should not be disqualified from purchasing the immovable property under any law at the time of sale, for example: under section 136 of the Act, a judge, a legal practitioner or an officer of the court is incompetent for purchase of actionable claim.
3. The buyer may be a natural person / judicial person, for example: a corporation or other legal person.

2. Subject Matter: – The sale under Transfer of Property Act, 1882 specifically deals with the sale of immovable property. Immovable property includes the benefits from the land and the things attached to the earth and it does not include standing timber, growing crops and grass.

3. Competency: – A valid sale requires both the parties i.e., the buyer and seller to be competent on the date of sale.

4. Money Consideration: – The consideration must only be in money to constitute a sale. If it is for exchange or some other items then it is not sale. The consideration for the sale must be paid, partly paid, promised or partly promised. Therefore price is money but not necessarily money immediately paid in notes and coins, it includes money which might be already due or payable at a future date.

5. Conveyance: – Section 54 provides for two ways for transfer of property: –

Where the property transferred is tangible immovable property of value of one hundred rupees and upward transfer can only be made by a registered instrument. Where the property is immovable property of less than one hundred rupees, it can be transferred either by registered instrument or delivery of property. The delivery of tangible immovable property occurs when the seller puts the buyer or such person as the buyer directs in possession of the property.

6. Registration of sale deed: – Where the value of tangible immovable property is Rs. 100 or more, the sale of such property requires registration of the deed. Where the property is intangible immovable property of any valuation, it will require registration to complete the sale.

7. Transfer of Ownership: – Ownership is the aggregation of all rights and liabilities in a property. When transfer of ownership occurs, all rights and liabilities in the property is transferred from transferor to transferee.

Rights and liabilities of Buyer and Seller

The buyer and the seller of the immovable property respectively are subject to the liabilities, and have the rights, mentioned in the rules following: –

Sec. 55 of the Transfer of property Act deals with the rights and liabilities of buyer and seller.

The buyer's rights and liabilities are divided into two stages:

- Before of completion of Sale and
- After completion

BUYER'S RIGHTS

1. **Before Completion of Sale:**

   a. A charge on the property for the purchase of money properly paid by him in anticipation of the delivery. This charge is converse of the seller's charge for unpaid price.
   b. Interest on such purchase money.
   c. The money and costs awarded to him in a suit for specific performance of the contract or to obtain a decree for its recession.

2. **After Completion of Sale:**

   After completion i.e., where ownership has passed to him.

a. The buyer is entitled to the benefits of any improvement or increase in value of the property.
b. Rents and profits thereof.

BUYER'S LIABILITIES

1. **Before Completion of Sale**

The buyer is bound:

a. To disclose to the seller any fact as to the nature or extent of the seller's interest in the property which the seller is not aware. This duty is like the seller's duty to disclose material defects in the property.
b. To pay or tender the purchase money to the seller or to such person as he directs.

2. After Completion of Sale:

a. To bear any loss arising from destruction, injury or decrease in value of the property.
b. To pay public charge and rents which may become payable in respect of the property.

SELLER'S RIGHTS

1. **Before Completion of Sale:**

The seller is entitled to rents and profits till the ownership passes to the buyer. If the buyer takes possession before completion of the sale, the seller has a right to claim interest on the unpaid purchase money from the date of possession.

2. After CompletionofSale:

The seller is entitled to a charge upon the property in the hands of-

a. The buyer or
b. Any transferee without consideration, or
c. Any transferee with notice of non-payment, for the amount of the unpaid purchase-money.

SELLER'S LIABILITIES

1. **Before Completion of Sale**

a. To produce to the buyer on his request for examination all documents relating to the property. The buyer must inspect the title deeds in his own interest, as otherwise, he may be fixed with constructive notice of matters which he could have discovered the title.
b. To the best of information, all relevant questions put to him.
c. On payment or tender of the price, to execute a proper conveyance of the property.
d. Between the date of the contract of sale and the delivery of the property, to take proper care of the property.
e. To pay compensation to the buyer if there is any loss or damages to the property.
f. To pay all public charges and rent accrued due in respect of the property, up to the date of the sale. Public charges means Government Revenue, Municipal Taxes, etc.

2. **After Completion of Sale:**

a. To give to the buyer or such person as he directs such possession of property as its nature admits. Actual possession is not possible in the case of incorporeal rights such as a right to fishery, etc.
b. Where the whole of the purchase money has been paid to the seller he is also bound to deliver to the buyer all documents of title. The cost of obtaining the deeds should be borne by the seller.

Difference between Sale under Transfer of Property Act and Contract for Sale

SALE

1.There is a transfer of ownership of the property.

2.Gives legal title to buyer.

3.Creates a right in rem.

4.Registration is mandatory where the sale is of immovable property of Rs. 100 or more.

CONTRACT FOR SALE

1. There is an agreement between the parties for the sale of the property with consent.

2. Does not generate any interest in the property.

3.Creates a right in personam

4. Registration is not required.

Nahar Lal vs. Brijnath 1928 AC 385

In this case, the court held that if the registration is done in violation of the provisions of the Registration Act, a document cannot be said to be duly registered.

Umakanta Das vs. Pradip Kumar Ray, AIR 1983 Ori 196

In this case, the court held that if the sale deed contains a condition that the price will be paid within one year, provided that possession is obtained within that time, and if possession is not obtained, the payment of the price will be postponed, or in the event of the vendee not getting the property, the price will not be paid. In all the above cases, the deed within the meaning of the section is the sale deed.

Raheja Universal Ltd. vs. NAC Ltd., 2012 4 SCC 148

In this case, the court states that a contract for sale of immovable property or an agreement to sell is a contract that a sale of such property shall be on the terms settled between the parties. This in itself does not create any interest or charge on such property.

Misabul Enterprises vs. Vijaya Srivastava, AIR 2003 Del. 15.

In this case, the court held that a contract of sale should be based on a mutual agreement between seller and buyer.

XXI
MORTGAGE

A mortgage is a transfer of an interest in specific immovable property as a security for the repayment of debt.

Justice Mahmud observed: "Mortgage, as understood in this country, cannot be defined better than by the definition adopted by the legislature in section 58, TPA."

The Supreme Court in **Kedar Lal v. Hari Lal** observed that the whole law of mortgage in India is embodied in the TPA read with Order 34 Rules 1 to 15 of CPC which deals with suits relating to mortgages of immovable property. It is important to note that the court cannot travel beyond these statutory provisions.

Section 58(a) of TPA defines the terms 'mortgage', 'mortgagor', 'mortgagee', 'mortgage-money', and 'mortgage-deed'.

Clause (a) of Section 58 reads:

A **mortgage** is the transfer of an interest in specific immovable property for the purpose of securing the payment of money advanced or to be advanced by way of loan, an existing or future debt, or the performance of an engagement that may give rise to a pecuniary liability.

The transferor is called a **mortgagor**, the transferee a **mortgagee**; the principal money and interest of which payment is secured for the time being are called the **mortgage-money**, and the instrument (if any) by which the transfer is effected is called a **mortgage-deed**.

Essential conditions of a Mortgage:

- There is a transfer of interest to the mortgagee.
- The interest created in specific immovable property.

- The mortgage should be supported by consideration.

Kinds of Mortgage
1.*Simple Mortgage [Section 58(b)]*

Simple mortgage.—Where, without delivering possession of the mortgaged property, the mortgagor binds himself personally to pay the mortgage-money, and agrees, expressly or impliedly, that, in the event of his failure to pay according to his contract, the mortgagee shall have a right to cause the mortgaged property to be sold and the proceeds of sale to be applied, so far as may be necessary, in payment of the mortgage money, the transaction is called a **simple mortgage** and the mortgagee a **simple mortgagee**.

The basic elements of a simple mortgage are:

- The mortgagor must have bound himself personally to repay the loan;
- The possession of the property is not given to the mortgagee; and
- To secure the loan he has transferred to the mortgage the right to have the specific immovable property sold in the event of his failure to repay.

Mathai Mathai v Joseph Mary

A certain property was mortgaged as collateral security for stridhan. The mortgagor was supposed to pay interest towards repayment of the loan amount. However, the deed did not consist of any provision about the delivery of possession and thus, the court held that such deed was to be considered as a simple mortgage.

Kishan Lai v Ganga Ram

The court reinstated that under section 58 (b) of the Transfer Of Property Act, 1882 the words "right to cause the property to be sold" implies that such power of sale can not be exercised by the mortgagee arbitrarily and requires the intervention of the court.

2.*Mortgage by Conditional Sale [Section 58(c)]*

Mortgage by conditional sale.—Where, the mortgagor ostensibly sells the mortgaged property— on condition that on default of payment of the mortgage money on a certain date the sale shall become absolute, or on condition that on such payment being made the sale shall become void, or on condition that on such payment being made the buyer shall transfer the property to the seller, the transaction is called mortgage by conditional sale and the mortgagee a mortgagee by conditional sale: Provided that no such transaction shall be deemed to be a mortgage unless the condition is embodied in the document which affects or purports to affect the sale.

Basic elements of a mortgage by conditional sale are:

- The mortgagor must ostensibly sell the property to the mortgagee.
- There must be a condition on such sale that either, on the repayment of the debt on a certain date.
- The sale shall become void or the buyer shall transfer the property to the seller, or in default of payment on the agreed date, the sale shall become absolute.
- The condition must be contained in the same document.

If the mortgagee makes any default on repayment of the debt (if the loan is not repaid), the sale would become **absolute and binding**, or

If the mortgagee does not make any default in the payment (repayment of the debt has been made), the sale would become **void**, or

If the mortgagee makes the payment, the buyer shall transfer the mortgaged property to the seller (the mortgagor shall transfer the property back to the mortgagee), such a transaction is called a **mortgage by conditional sale.**

However, it is to be noted that no such transaction will be considered to be a mortgage where no condition is mentioned in the same document which shall affect the sale.

Rama v Samiyappa

The court held that an essential element of this form of mortgage is that on default of payment the mortgaged property becomes the absolute property of the mortgagee and there is no personal liability for the repayment of the debt on the part of the mortgagor.

3. *Usufructuary Mortgage [Section 58(d)]*

Usufructuary mortgage.—Where the mortgagor delivers possession or expressly or by implication binds himself to deliver possession of the mortgaged property to the mortgagee and authorises him to retain such possession until payment of the mortgage-money, and to receive the rents and profits accruing from the property or any part of such rents and profits and to appropriate the same in lieu of interest, or payment of the mortgage-money, or partly in lieu of interest partly in payment of the mortgage money, the transaction is called a **usufructuary mortgage** and the mortgagee a **usufructuary mortgagee.**

The basic elements of usufructuary mortgage are:

- The mortgagor either delivers possession or expressly or impliedly binds himself to deliver possession of the mortgaged property to the mortgagee.
- The mortgagor authorises the mortgagee till the payment of the mortgage money is satisfied:

1.to retain such possession;

2. to receive the rents and profits or any part of such rents and profits arising from the property

- to appropriate such rents and profits in lieu of interest, or payment of the mortgage money, or partly in payment of the mortgage money.

In **Hikmatulla v Imam Ali**

The court held that the mortgagee is entitled to hold on to the mortgaged property until the money due is fully paid. The time period for payment of the due amount is never fixed in Usufructuary Mortgage and if such time period is mentioned it ceases to be a Usufructuary mortgage.

Chathu v Kunjan

The court held that there is no personal liability of the mortgagor involved to repay the mortgage amount and thus he can not be personally sued for the same.

4. *English Mortgage [Section 58(e)]*

English mortgage.—Where the mortgagor binds himself to repay the mortgage money on a certain date, and transfers the mortgaged property absolutely to the mortgagee, but subject to a proviso that he will re-transfer it to the mortgagor upon payment of the mortgage-money as agreed, the transaction is called an **English mortgage.**

Basic elements of an English mortgage are:

- There is a consensus to pay the amount on the due date. The mortgagor has to repay the mortgage money on the due date.
- There is an absolute transfer of property to the mortgagee.
- Such absolute transfer needs to be subject to a proviso that the mortgagee will transfer the property to the mortgagor upon payment of mortgage money on the agreed date.

In the case of English Mortgage, the mortgagor transfers the ownership of the mortgaged property absolutely to the mortgagee as security. The mortgagee shall return or re-transfer the property once the mortgagor repays the amount as agreed on a particular date.

Narayan v Venkatarama

The court held that the English mortgage has three essential ingredients, which are –

- The mortgagor is personally bound to repay the money
- The property to the mortgagee is transferred absolutely
- The property will be transferred back once the dues have been settled.

5. *Mortgage by deposit of title deeds (Equitable Mortgage) [Section 58(f)]*

Mortgage by deposit of title-deeds.—Where a person in any of the following towns, namely, the towns of Calcutta, Madras, and Bombay, and in any other town which the State Government concerned may, by notification in the Official Gazette, specify in this behalf, delivers to a creditor or his agent documents of title to immovable property, with intent to create a security thereon, the transaction is called a **mortgage by deposit of title-deeds.**

In English Law, this type of mortgage is called an 'equitable mortgage' as opposed to a 'legal mortgage' because there is just a deposit of a document of the title without writing or without any other additional formalities. The intention of the legislature in providing such a mortgage is to give facilities to the mercantile community in situations where it may be necessary to raise money all of a sudden before any opportunity of preparing a mortgage deed can be afforded. Thus, this type of mortgage does not require any writing, and being an oral transaction is not affected by the Law of Registration.

The basic elements of this type of mortgage are:

- There must be a debt.
- There must be a deposit/delivery of the title deeds.
- There is an intention that the deeds shall be security for the debt; and
- Territorial restrictions

It is important to note that such a mortgage can be made only in certain areas and not everywhere in India. The said restriction to certain areas means the place where the deeds are to be delivered and not the situation of the property mortgaged. Also, a deposit of deeds beyond that area will neither create a mortgage nor an exchange.

United Bank Of India v Messra Lekharam Sonam and Co.

The court held that mere submission of the title deed with regard to the property is the only essential necessary for it to be considered as a security. There is no other additional requirement.

6. *Anomalous Mortgage [Section 58(g)]*

Anomalous mortgage.—A mortgage that is not a simple mortgage, a mortgage by conditional sale, a usufructuary mortgage, an English mortgage, or a mortgage by deposit of title deeds within the meaning of this section is called an anomalous mortgage.

Hathika v Puthiya Purayil Padmanathan

A mortgagor borrowed a certain amount from the mortgagee and such property was also handed over to him. The mortgage amount was to be paid within a period of 6 months failing which the mortgagee had the right to sell the property and realize the amount. Though the document described it as a usufructuary mortgage the court held it to be an anomalous mortgage as it had characters of simple mortgage as well as Usufructuary mortgage.

Rights of Mortgagor

1. Right of Redemption

- As per Section 60 of the Transfer of the Property Act, 1882 one of the important rights of the mortgagor is the right to redeem the mortgage.
- Once the money has become due on the specified date the mortgagor has the right to get back the mortgaged property on paying the money to the mortgagee.
- Right to redemption is a statutory and legal right which cannot be extinguished on the entering into any agreement.

2. Right to transfer to a third party

- As per Section 60A of the Transfer of Property Act, 1882 the mortgagor may direct the mortgagee to assign the mortgage debt and authorise him to transfer the property to a third party instead of transferring him the same.
- The object of this section is to enable the mortgagor to pay off the debt of the mortgagee by taking a loan from another person on the security of

the same property.

3. Right to inspection and production of documents

- As per Section 60B of the Transfer of Property Act, 1882 the mortgagor may inspect anytime the document of title relating to the mortgaged property which is in the custody of the mortgagee.
- The costs and expenses incurred while inspecting the documents may be borne by the mortgagee.

4. Right to accession

As per Section 63 of the Transfer of Property Act, 1882 during the subsistence of the mortgage if any accession is made to the mortgaged property where the property is in possession of the mortgagor itself and then the mortgagor has a right to take in accession after the redemption of the mortgage.

Accession can be of two types:

- Natural accession.
- Acquired accession.
- Right to improvement

As per Section 63A of the Transfer of Property Act, 1882 during the subsistence of the mortgage if any improvement is made to the property where the property is in possession of the mortgagee and then the mortgagor has a right to take the improvements made to the property upon the redemption.

But where the improvements were at cost of the mortgage by preserving the property from destruction then the mortgagor is liable to pay the cost which is incurred by the mortgagee in preserving the property.

5. Right to a renewed lease

As per Section 64 of the Transfer of Property Act, 1882 where the property which the mortgagor has given for mortgage is a leasehold property if the mortgagee renews the leases during the subsistence of mortgage the mortgagor shall obtain the benefit of the lease upon the redemption of the mortgage.

6. Right to grant a lease

As per Section 65A of the Transfer of Property Act, 1882 a mortgagor shall have the right to grant a lease of which is lawfully in possession with the mortgagee and such lease shall be binding on the mortgagee subject to the following conditions:

- Lease shall be according to the local laws, custom or usages.
- No rent or premium shall be paid in advance.
- The lease shall not contain a covenant for renewal.
- The lease shall come into effect within six months from the date on which it is made.
- In case lease of buildings, the duration of the lease shall not exceed not more than three years.

Liabilities of Mortgagor

Section 65 and 66 of the Transfer of the Property Act, 1882 deals with the liabilities of the mortgagor.

Section 65 is the implied liabilities which are laid upon the mortgagor. Subject to the contrary, every mortgagor is deemed to have made the following covenant.

a. Covenant for title

As per Section 65(a) of the Transfer of the Property Act, 1882 there is an implied covenant that the mortgagor transferring the interest in the property to the mortgagee belongs to the mortgagor only.

And it is necessary that the mortgagor possess the transferable interest in the property.

In case mortgagor makes a breach in the covenant the mortgagor is liable to compensate.

b. Covenant for the defence of the title

As per Section 65(b) of the Transfer of the Property Act, 1882 the mortgagor has a duty impliedly to either defend the title if anyone tries to take away the title from the mortgagee or help the mortgagee in defending the title.

By doing so, the mortgagor bears all the expenses incurred while defending the title.

c. Covenant for payment of public charge

As per Section 65(c) of the Transfer of the Property Act, 1882 there is an implied duty to the mortgagor that upon the execution of the mortgage the mortgagor shall pay all the necessary changes.

If the mortgagor fails to meet the required charges the property would be sold by the public authorities and realise the charges.

d. Covenant for payment of rent

As per Section 65(d) of the Transfer of the Property Act, 1882 where the property mortgaged by the mortgagor is a leasehold property there is an implied duty of the mortgagor to pay the rent of the mortgaged property.

e. Covenant for the discharge of prior mortgage

As per Section 65(e) of the Transfer of the Property Act, 1882 there is implied duty of the mortgagor to discharge the prior mortgage if any.

There is always a presumption that the mortgagor has a covenant with the subsequent mortgages to pay off the mortgage on becoming due.

In such subsequent mortgage if the mortgagor makes a breach the subsequent mortgagee would have the right to sue for his mortgaged money.

Rights of Mortgagee

1. Right to foreclosure or sale

As per Section 67 of the Transfer of Property Act, 1882 the mortgagee has a right to foreclosure or sale. When the mortgagor does not pay the mortgage money after the specified date is over and the mortgagor's right to redeem the mortgaged money has become complete but he has failed to avail that right then mortgagee gets a right to institute suit for a decree that the mortgagor is absolutely debarred of his right to redeem the property. The difference between the right to redemption and right to foreclosure is that the former is an absolute right whereas the right to foreclose is not. The mortgagor cannot limit the right of redemption but the right to foreclose can be made subject to a contract between the parties.

2. Right to sue

As per Section 68 of the Transfer of Property Act, 1882 the mortgagee has every right to sue for the mortgaged money. The mortgagee can sue for mortgaged money in the following circumstances:

- where mortgagor binds himself to repay the money to the mortgagee.
- where the property mortgaged by the mortgagee has been destroyed either wholly or partially without the fault of the mortgagee.
- where the property mortgaged, the mortgagee is deprived of the security due to some wrongful act done by the mortgagor.
- where the mortgagors fail to deliver the possession to the mortgagee.

3. Right to sell

- As per Section 69 of the Transfer of Property Act, 1882 the mortgagee has every right to sell the mortgaged property if the mortgaged money has not been received
- This right can be exercised by the mortgagee when the mortgagor makes a default in payment of the mortgaged money after the specified date is over.
- This right can be exercised without the intervention of the court but only in the following cases:
- if the mortgage is an English mortgage both the mortgagor and mortgage should not be Hindu, Muslim, Buddhist, or a member of any other race as specified by the state government;
- when there is a contract between the mortgagor and mortgagee the sale would take place without the intervention of the court in case of default in payment of mortgaged money;
- to exercise the above right the mortgaged property should be situated either in Calcutta, Madras, Bombay, Ahmedabad, Kanpur, Allahabad, Lucknow, Coimbatore, Cochin and Delhi.

Liabilities of Mortgagee

As per Section 76 of the Transfer of Property Act, 1882 list down the duties of the mortgagee who is in possession of the property which belongs to the mortgagor.

The duties mentioned under are the statutory duties except for the duties which are mentioned under clauses (c) and (d) the duties under these clauses are mentioned in the contract by the parties.

Duty to manage the property

1. The mortgagee has a duty to take reasonable care in the property of the mortgagor.
2. Though he has a liability to take reasonable care in the property the mortgagee is not bound by the directions given by the mortgagor and the mortgagee has acquired absolute rights in managing the property.
3. The only condition which is put forward by the mortgagor is that he cannot lease the property beyond the termination of his interest in the mortgaged property.

Duty to collect rents and profits

1. The mortgagee who is in possession of the mortgagor's property can collect the rent and profits arising from the property.
2. One outstanding feature of usufructuary mortgagee is the rent and profits collected from the property are appropriated by the mortgagee instead of payment of interest.
3. Mortgagee becomes liable for the collection of rent and profit only to the property which he is liable to acquire the rent and profits and not liable for the whole rental property.

Duty to pay rent, revenue and public charges

1. If there is an agreement between the mortgagor and mortgagee that the mortgagee has to pay the rents, revenue, taxes and outgoings then the mortgagee is liable to pay all of them which have been agreed by him.
2. The mortgagee is not allowed to take the benefits without paying the taxes etc.
3. In case the money which has been obtained from the property is insufficient for paying the charges, he may pay out of his own pocket and later add the amount which has been paid by him to the debit account.

Duty to make necessary repairs

1. If there is an agreement between the mortgagor and mortgagee that the mortgagee is bound to carry out all the necessary repairs in the property then the mortgagee is liable to take care of the necessary repairs.
2. The necessary repairs in the property are to be made only when there is a surplus amount from the rents and profits.

Duty not to commit any destructive act

1. While the property is in the mortgagee's possession he is prevented from committing any act which is either in destructive nature or is injurious to the mortgaged property.
2. He is prohibited from carrying out any acts which may result in reducing the value of the property.
3. If the property is destroyed because of acts of god then the mortgagee is not liable for the property.

Duty towards the proper use of insurance money

1. Where the mortgaged property has been insured against loss by fire it is the duty of the mortgagee to apply for the insurance money in restoring the property.
2. The mortgagee is also bound to apply the money received under the insurance policy in reinstating the property.
3. The property which is to be insured only for the two-third of its value.

Duty to keep the accounts

1. The mortgagee has a statutory duty under this provision in keeping the correct accounts of all incomes arose and expenses incurred by the mortgagee.
2. The only exception is when the mortgagee is entitled to adjust the income against the interest he is not allowed to give full accounts because something there may be no money left to use for other expenses.

Duty to apply rents and profit

This clause provides the manner in which the mortgagee who is in possession of the property has to apply for rents and profits during the mortgage.

Charge

According to **Section 100** of the Transfer of Property Act, 1882 Charge means where the immovable property is transferred by one party to another party for the security of payment of money. The transaction does not amount to a mortgage and all the provisions which are applicable to simple mortgages shall apply to the charge. The charge does not transfer any interest in favour of the charge holder but he has the right to recover his money from the property.

Essential under Section 100 of Transfer of Property Act, 1882:

1. A charge can be created either by an act of parties or through the operation of law.
2. It is created as a security for payment of money.
3. The transaction which is created does not amount to a mortgage.
4. A charge can be enforced by a suit.

5. A charge may be extinguished either by an act of parties by way of the release of debt or by a novation or by a merger.

XXII

LEASE

Section 105 states the definition of a lease which states that it is a transfer of immovable property for a particular time period for a consideration of which the transferee has accepted the terms surrounding the agreement.

What are the essentials of a lease?

Parties must be competent: The parties in a lease agreement should be competent to enter into a contract. Lesser should be entitled to a property and have absolute rights over that property.

Right of possession: Ownership rights are not transferred in a lease, only the possession of the property is transferred.

Rent: Consideration for a lease can be taken in the form of a rent or premium.

Acceptance: Lessee, who is to get the interest in the property after lease, has to accept the lease agreement along with the time period and terms & conditions imposed on the transfer.

Time Period: Lease always takes place for a particular time period which is to be specified in the lease agreement. It can be relaxed at the option of the lessor.

What happens when the lease agreement does not prescribe the time period of the lease?

Section 106 provides for the duration of the lease in the absence of the lease agreement. It lays down that in the absence of a contract, lease can be ended by both parties to the lease by issuing a notice to quit. The prescribed time period always commences from the date of receiving the notice to quit. Following are the circumstances:

1. When a lease for Agricultural or manufacturing purpose is deemed to be of year to year, then it will attract a 6-month notice that the lease will end on the expiry of 1 year from the date of the commencement of the lease.
2. When a lease for any other purpose is deemed to be of the month to month, then it will attract a 15-day notice that the lease will end on the expiry of 1 month from the commencement of the lease.

There is proviso to this section which states that the notice to quit in this section should be written and conveyed to the party who is required to abide by it. If this is not possible then it should be attached to a conspicuous place in that property.

How is a lease executed?

Section 107 states about lease how made. This section covers three aspects:

When there is a lease of Immovable property for a term of 1 year or more – This can only be made by a registered deed.

All other leases of Immovable property – Can be either made by a registered deed or an oral agreement or settlement along with the transfer of possession of that property.

When the lease is of multiple properties that require multiple deeds, it will be made by both the parties of the lease.

In the case of **Punjab National Bank v. Ganga Narain Kapur**, Court held that if the lease is done through an oral agreement, then the provisions of Section 106 will apply.

Rights and liabilities of Lessor and lessee

1. Rights of the lessor are

- A lessor has a right to recover the rent from the lease which was mentioned in the lease agreement.
- Lessor has a right to take back the possession of his property from the lessee if the lessee commits any breach of condition.
- Lessor has a right to recover the amount of damages from the lessee if there is any damage done to the property.
- Lessor has a right to take back the possession of his property from the lessee on the termination of the lease term prescribed in the agreement.

2. Liabilities of the lessor

- The lessor has to disclose any material defect relating to the property which the lessee does not know and cannot with ordinary supervision find out.
- Lessor is bound by the request of the lessee to give him the right of possession over his property.
- Lessor can enter into a contract with the lessee if he agrees to abide by all terms and conditions prescribed in the agreement, he can enjoy the property for the rest of the time period without any interference with an obligation to pay the rent later on.

3. Rights of the lessee

- Lessee has the right to deduct any expenses he has made for repairs in the property from the rent if the lessor has failed to in reasonable time.
- Lessee has a right to recover any such payment which a lessor is bound to make by can deducting it from the interest of the rent or directly from the lessor. He has this right when the lessor has neglected to make that required payment.
- Lessee has a right to detach all things that he may have attached in the property or earth. His only obligation is that he has to leave the property in the same condition as he received it.
- When a lease is of unspecified duration in the lease agreement, lessee or his legal representative have a right to collect all the profits or benefits from the crops which were sown by the lessee at that property. They also have a right of free ingress and egress from such property even if the lease ends.
- Lessee has a right to transfer absolutely the property or any part of his interest in that property by sub-leasing or through mortgaging. Lessee is not independent of the terms and conditions mentioned in the lease agreement.

4. Liabilities of the lessee

- Lessee is under an obligation to disclose all related material facts which are likely to increase the value of the property for which the lessee has an interest in and the lessor is not aware of.
- Lessee is under an obligation to pay the rent or premium which is settled upon in the agreement to the lessor or his agent within the prescribed

time.

- Lessee is under an obligation to maintain the property in the condition that he initially got the property on commencement of the lease and he has to return it in the same condition.
- If lessee gets to know about any proceedings relating to the property or any encroachment or any interference, then lessee is under an obligation to give notice to the lessor.
- Lessee has a right to use all the assets and goods which are on the property as an owner would use which is preserving it to the best of its nature. He is although under obligation to prevent any other person from using that asset or good for any other purpose from what was prescribed in the lease agreement.
- The lessee cannot attach any permanent structure without the consent of the lessor except for the purpose of agriculture.
- Lessee is under an obligation to give the possession of the property back to the lessor after the expiry of the prescribed term of the lease.

How does a Lease end?

Section 111 states about the determination of the lease, which lays down the ways in which lease is terminated:

Lapse of time – When the prescribed time of the lease expires, the lease is terminated.

Specified event – When there is a condition on time of lease depending upon a happening of an event.

Interest – Lessor's interest to lease the property may cease, hence resulting in the termination of the lease.

Same owner – When the interest of both lessor and lessee are transferred or vested in the same person.

Express Surrender – This happens when the lessee ceases to have an interest in the property and comes into a mutual agreement with the lessor.

Implied Surrender – When the lessee enters into a contract with another for the lease of property, this is an implied surrender of the existing lease.

Forfeiture – There are three ways by which a lease can be terminated:

- When there is a breach of an express condition by the lessee. The lessor may get the possession of the property back.

- When lessee renounces his character or gives the title of the property to a third person.
- When the lessee is termed as insolvent by the banks, and if the conditions provide for it, the lease will stand terminated.

Expiry of Notice to Quit – When the notice to quit by the lessor to the lessee expires, the lease will also expire.

What is notice to quit and what happens after it?

Notice to quit is a formal written statement that is issued to the lessee if the lessor desires to end the lease agreement, whether on the expiry of the duration as stated under Section 106 or on grounds specified in Section 111.

Any lease can be forfeited as mentioned in the sub-clause (g) of Section 111, by acceptance of the notice to quit.

But **Section 112**, states that if the lessor after initiating the process of termination of the lease on the grounds of forfeiture accepts any rent from the lessee, it will be understood that the lease will still exist and the termination and notice to quit has been waived.

Section 113 provides two ways in which the notice can be waived, that is expressly or impliedly.

Express Waiver of notice to quit – When a lessor accepts the rent from the lessee after the notice to quit has been served, this is called express waiver of notice to quit.

Implied Waiver of notice to quit – When a lessor issues notice to quit to the lessee, and upon expiry of that notice, lesser issues another notice to quit to the lessee. The first notice to quit is impliedly waived.

Waiver of notice also shows the intention to continue the existing lease.

Effect of Holding over

Section 116 states about the effect of holding overlays down that if there has been a waiver of notice to quit, it will not be called a new lease instead it will be called as a lease on sufferance or tolerance without objecting against it. The term 'Holding over' stands for retained possession of a property which has been leased. After this, the lease is renewable as any normal lease and in the way prescribed in Section 106.

This section provides that if the lessor agrees to the holding over of the property by the lessee, it will be renewed. But if the lessor does not entertain the retained possession by the lessee, he can initiate suit proceedings against him on grounds of trespass or tenant at sufferance.

XXIII

EXCHANGE

Section 118 of the Transfer of Property Act, 1882 – when two people mutually transfer the ownership of one thing for the ownership of another, the transaction is called an 'exchange' when neither thing or both things are money only. A transfer of property at the completion of an exchange can take place only in the manner provided for the transfer of such property by sale.

The transaction is called an **exchange** when the ownership of one thing for the ownership of another is mutually exchanged by two parties, neither thing or both things being money only. It is a transaction in which each party acquires property in which it previously had no interest. There must be a physical delivery of the property to the parties for a valid exchange, and each party to the exchange has the rights and is subject to the seller's liability as to what he gives, and also has the rights and liabilities of the buyer as to what he takes.

ESSENTIALS OF AN EXCHANGE

1. There must be a minimum of two parties and two properties, one each belonging to each of them;
2. A mutual transfer of these properties has to take place, i.e. A to transfer his property to B and B to transfer his property to A;
3. Property can be exchanged for property that is either movable or immovable.
4. Besides these properties, no other consideration should be involved.

Mutual Exchange

The term 'mutually' indicates that the parties need to be the same and two things need to be exchanged. A transfers his property to B, for instance, and B transfers his own property in return for A. It is not an exchange if the transfer is just from the hand of one of the parties. In the discharge of her maintenance claim, a transfer by a husband to a wife is not an exchange, as the wife does not transfer the possession of something. Similarly, a document in which one decree is set off against another and the balance made up by the transfer of land is not an exchange, since two items are not mutually transferred.

The object of exchange must be lawful

The object of exchange must not be unlawful. Exchange is primarily a contract, and if the object is unlawful or aims at defeating the provisions of law, it will be invalid. A deed of exchange to compromise criminal proceedings between the parties was executed in Srihari Jena v. Khetramohun Jaina. The agreement between them specified that the deed of exchange could not be taken from the Registrar's Office until the proceedings had been compromised. The court held that the exchange was not valid in light of section 23 of the Indian Contract Act, 1872.

In **John Thomas v Joseph Thomas**

Whether the written agreement for the mutual exchange of properties amounted to a sale or an exchange was the question before the court. The parties had known each other for a long time. One of the parties, A, owned property X, while the other party, B, owned property Y. Since X was more valuable than Y, B paid an additional amount of one lakh rupees towards equalization money when A exchanged X for Y. The court held that it amounted to a sale and not an exchange, because money had been paid from one party to another.

RIGHT OF A PARTY DEPRIVED OF THING RECEIVED IN EXCHANGE; [Section 119]

If any party to an exchange or any person claiming through or under such party is by reason of any defect in the title of the other party deprived of the thing or part of the thing received by him in exchange , then, unless a contrary intention appears from the terms of the exchange , such other party is liable to him or any person claiming through or under him for loss caused thereby, or at the option of the person so deprived for the return of thing transferred , if still in the possession of such other party or his legal representative or a transferee from him without consideration.

According to this section, each party is entitled to the property to which it was entitled under the contract and provides the aggrieved party with a remedy in the case that it does not receive what it was supposed to obtain under that contract.

Example : A and B, enter into a contract to mutually exchange their X and Y properties, respectively. A supplies X to B, but B fails to supply Y to A. In accordance with the rules laid down in this section, A's rights will be determined. It provides the party so dispossessed in the alternative with two remedies:

i) He can seek compensation for the loss of such dispossession caused to him.

(ii) He is entitled to take back the property he has transferred. This right may be exercised as against:

(a) The other party to the exchange in whose hands there is possession;

(b) Where the possession is kept by the transferee's legal representative;

(c) Where the possession is with the other party's gratuitous transferee.

Ramsayivan v Lalji Ram, 1941

An exchange of land took place between A and the predecessor of B, but B sold the same illegally to a third party in 1988. It was decided that the purchaser of the land would not have any locus standi to say anything about the exchange nor that of A's title. The principle of getting the property in return in the case of deprivation of the exchanged property also extends to cases where there is no transfer at all instead of subsequent deprivation of the transferred property. If a party to an exchange fails to acquire possession of the property it is entitled to obtain in exchange, it shall also be entitled, at his option, to the return of the assets which it has exchanged.

Jattu Ram V. Hakama Singh

Due to false entries made by patwari, there was a defect in the title of land obtained by one party for exchange and the party was deprived of some portion of the land as per Deed of Exchange. It was held by the Supreme Court that entries made in the official records by patwari do not generate title, so to the extent that the opposite party was liable to return land (property).

The provisions of **Section 119** shall apply only in situations where one of the parties to the Transaction has been deprived of the things/property transferred because of a defect in the title of another person transferring the things/property.

Example: Assume that Mr. A and Mr. B were transferred ownership of their residential property and Mr. C's brother, Mr. A, was forcibly disposed of Mr. B's possession of residential property, the ownership of which was transferred in exchange to Mr. B.

RIGHTS AND LIABILITIES OF PARTIES TO THE EXCHANGE (Section 120)

The rights and liabilities of the parties to the exchange are not expressly stated in section 120. It just provides that each party has the rights and is subject to a seller's liabilities as to what he gives and has rights and is subject to a buyer's liabilities as to what he takes. The rights and liabilities of the parties in the event of an exchange are therefore the same as in the case of a sale. One thing is given in return and another thing has been taken, so parties play the role of both seller and buyer. The rules of the Sale of Goods Act 1930 are also applicable in exchange for movable property.

In exchange, all parties have equal rights over one another. He is considered to be in the role of a seller when the person transfers the property to the other and he holds all the rights that a seller has when selling property. The person who receives the property is called a buyer and, because of being a buyer, he has all the privileges that a buyer possesses.

EXCHANGE OF MONEY (Section 121)

On an exchange of money, each party thereby warrants the genuineness of the money given by him. Money can be exchanged with money, of the same or different denominations or even different currencies. The term money here includes not only coins, but also currency notes.

XXIV

GIFT

According to **Section 122** of the Transfer of Property Act (TPA), a transfer of movable or immovable property, which is already in existence, without consideration is a gift. Such a transfer should be made voluntarily by the transferor. The acceptance of the gift should be made by the person to whom the transfer is made or on behalf of him.

Parties

There parties to a gift are:

- **Donor** – The person who is donating or transferring his property in return for no consideration is a donor (transferor).
- **Donee** – The person for whom a donation or gift is made is a donee. In simple words, the receiver of the gift is the donee (Transferee).

Types of property

Section 122 of the TPA defines a gift as a transfer of 'movable' or 'immovable' property. Property thus can be divided into two categories: movable and; immovable. What is movable and immovable property?

1. Immovable property

As the name itself suggests, immovable property is a property that cannot be moved. Things like buildings, walls, walls, trees, land, benefits arising out of the land, and things attached to the land are immovable property. The water tank attached with the house, doors, and windows are all immovable property.

2. Movable property

Anything that doesn't come under the category of 'Immovable property' is movable property. The name by itself defines the term: 'movable,' meaning that it can be moved.

Thus, anything which can be moved without damaging it is a movable property. Though the definition of movable property is not given in the TPA, section 3 of the said Act states a list of things that are movable properties. They are standing timber, growing crops or grass.

Though a tree is usually considered an immovable property, if it is grown for timber, it shall be considered a movable property as it can be cut down for other uses.

Modes of gifting

Gifting someone isn't that easy. For a gift to be recognized and valid, specific procedures should be followed. These procedures may vary according to the nature of the property. For instance, an immovable property has to be registered upon its transfer. But this is not the case for movable property.

The modes of how a transfer should be made are mentioned under **section 123** of TPA.

1. Immovable property

Gifting an immovable property should be made only by a registered instrument. This registered instrument should be signed by the donor himself or by any person signing on behalf of the donor. At Least two witnesses have to attest the instrument.

In the case of **Thulasimani Ammal vs. Commissioner Of Income Tax & Anr.**, the court held that mere handing over possession or handing over documents would not constitute a valid gift. The transfer of gifts has to be registered.

R.N. Dawar v. Ganga Ram Saran Dhama

In this case, it was held that the title of the immovable property could not be passed on to another person unless it is registered. Mere possession cannot confer the title to another if such a gift isn't registered.

2. Movable property

Gifting of a movable property doesn't have to be made through a registered instrument. Thus, it is possible to make a gift of movable property with or without a registered instrument and through delivery.

In the case of **Ms. Mayawati vs. Dy Commissioner Of Income-Tax**, it was held that mere gifting of the movable property voluntarily and delivering the possession of such property to the donee is enough for the gift to be valid.

Essential elements

Section 122 of TPA defines a gift as a voluntary transfer of property by one person to another without consideration. The donee should accept such gifts.

From the definition, we can conclude that the followings are the essential ingredients of gift:

1. A transfer of title or possession

First of all, there should be a transfer of ownership or title taking place. One person should do such a transfer to another person.

For immovable property, the transfer of title should be done with a registered instrument. Mere words stating that A's land is gifted by A to B is not enough. The transfer of immovable property should be effected through a registered instrument.

However, for movable property, transferring the title through a registered instrument or by way of transferring the possession is enough.

2. Existence of property

For a transfer of property to take place, there should be a property in existence. One cannot transfer a property that is not in his possession or ownership. Nor can he transfer a future property.

3. Voluntarily made

A gift is given without consideration. Thus, the beneficiary of such transfer is the donee. Thus a transfer of gift should be made voluntarily by the donor since he is the person who is at a loss.

The donor should have voluntarily made the gift without any coercion, fraud, misrepresentation, undue influence, or force. If a gift has been obtained through any one of the above-mentioned means, it can be said that such a gift has not been made voluntarily and hence declared void.

4. Without consideration

A gift is given out of love and concern. Thus it is given for free without any consideration. If such a transfer of property is made for any consideration, even for a corn piece, it shall be considered a transfer of property, sale, or exchange and not as gift. Thus a gift should be made purely without any consideration.

5. Acceptance

After the donor makes a gift to a donee, the transaction becomes complete only when the donee accepts it. If the donor doesn't accept it, then it is treated as if the gift isn't made.

Acceptance when to be made

Every gift which is gifted should be accepted by the donee for the transfer to become complete and valid. According to **Section 122** of the Act, the acceptance of a gift should be made while the donor is still capable of giving the gift and during the donor's lifetime. The donee should also accept the gift before he dies. If the donee dies before accepting such gift, then the gift becomes invalid (or void).

Is acceptance by donee essential for the validity of the gift?

Except in the case of Mohammedan law, the acceptance of a gift is essential for the validity of gift. A gift can be beneficial or a burden to a donee. Thus, a donee has to accept the gift for the gift to be valid.

The donee should accept the gift during the lifetime of the donor and while the donor is capable of giving it.

Where there are several gifts in several transactions, the donee can accept the ones with benefit and reject the ones with a burden. However, if all the gifts are given in a single transaction, he has to accept all or reject all. In either way, the donee's acceptance is a must.

Future property-gift

A gift can be made only with an existing property. **Section 124** of the TPA states that a gift of future property is void. Where a gift is made regarding an existing property and of future property, the existing property can be gifted but not the future / non-existing property. The property that is gifted or is to be gifted should be in existence on the day the transfer is made.

Gift to several donees

A donor can make a gift to a donee or several donees. According to **section 125** of TPA, if a gift is made to several donees and one donee doesn't accept it, it becomes void to the interest to which he would have taken if he had accepted it.

Example: If 10 lakh rupees is gifted by A to his daughters W, X, Y, and Z with 2.5 lakh each. Daughter Z refuses to accept it. In this case, the 2.5 lakh of daughter Z becomes void and goes back to father A. The remaining 7.5 lakh for the other three daughters becomes valid.

Revocation/suspension of gift

A gift is given by a person (donor) without any consideration. This doesn't mean that he can take back or cancel such a gift and take it back whenever he wishes. If he does so, the donee will get affected. Thus, a gift once made cannot be revoked or canceled except under few circumstances.

A gift can be revoked/suspended as mentioned under **section 126** only on the following grounds:

Where donor and donee have already agreed with the condition that the gift shall be revoked/suspended in the event of a specific event. However, such an event should not depend on the will of the donor. If the event is in the donor's will, then this gift is void wholly or partly, depending on the case.

Example 1: X gives a house to Y with the condition that he might take it back if Y or his descendants die before X. and Y agrees to this condition. Y dies without any descendants. The gift can go back to X.

In the above example, the special event is the death of Y and his descendants before X. This specified event is not under the control or will of the donor. Thus it is a valid gift.

Example 2: X gives to Y three houses, house A, house B, and house C, upon a condition that X will take back house C whenever he wants. Here, the gift of house A and B is valid. However, the gift of house C is not valid.

In the example mentioned above, the special event is 'taking back house C whenever X wants.' The action is under the control of X. Thus, the gift of house A and B is valid but not the gift of house C.

The second ground for a gift to be revoked/suspended is in the cases where it is allowed in a regular contract. For example, undue influence, misrepresentation, fraud are the grounds for revocation/suspension present in a contract. This can be the grounds in the case of gifts too.

Onerous gift

The term 'Onerous' means 'burdened with an obligation.' When a donor gifts a donee with a property, this may not always benefit the donee. The said gift may also contain certain obligations, which may be a burden for a donee.

Section 127 of the TPA deals with onerous gifts. Where a donee gifts a donor with several things in a single transaction, and one of them is a burden to the donee where the rest are beneficial to the donee, the donee can accept all (including the burdened property) or reject them all (including the property with benefits). He cannot accept the gifts with benefit and reject the ones with a burden.

In the case where a donor is gifting several things in two or more separate and individual transactions, of which one individual transaction is of burden, the donee can accept the gifts with benefits and reject the one with a burden.

Example 1: X has shares in company A running in difficulty, and company B, which is functioning successfully. X gifts all of his shares from both the companies to Y. Y cannot take shares from company B and refuse to accept the shares from A. Here, Y can either accept shares from both the company or reject them all.

Example 2: X has shares in company A which is running in difficulty, and company B, which is functioning successfully. X gifts the shares from company A and B in two separate and individual transactions to Y. Here, Y can refuse the shares from company A. This doesn't mean that he cannot accept the shares from company B. Y can refuse shares of A and get shares of B. This is because each transaction is done separately and individually.

To put it in simple words, if several things are gifted in a single transaction, the donee can either accept them all or reject them all. But if several things are given in several transactions, the donee can accept the ones that he likes and reject the ones that are a burden to him.

Universal Donee

Section 128 of TPA talks about universal donee. When a gift is gifted to a donee from a donor, and such gift consists of the donor's whole property, the donee becomes a universal donee. As the donee is gifted with the donor's whole property, the donee is liable to all the benefits and burdens that the donor holds. In this case, the donee is personally liable to pay all the debts and dues of the donor. This liability to pay back all the dues applies only to the extent of the property's value and not more than that.

Example: A gifts to B all his properties. The value of A's whole property is 10 million. However, if the debts and dues of A are 11 million, B is liable to pay only 10 million as the gift value is only 10 million. B doesn't have to pay back the remaining 1 million from his personal property.

Exceptions

Section 129 of the Act provides the gifts which are treated as exceptions to the whole chapter of gifts under the Act. These are:

- **Donations mortis causa**

These are gifts made in contemplation of death.

- **Muslim-gifts (Hiba)**

These are governed by the rules of Muslim Personal Law.

XXV
EASEMENT

Meaning and nature of Easements

The concept of easement has been defined under **Section 4** of The Indian Easements Act, 1882. According to the provisions of Section 4, an easementary right is a right possessed by the owner or occupier of the land on some other land, not his own, to provide the beneficial enjoyment of the land.

This right is granted because without the existence of this right an occupier or owner cannot fully enjoy his own property.

It includes the right to do or continue to do something or to prevent or to continue to prevent something in connection with or in respect of some other land, which is not his own, for the enjoyment of his own land.

The word **'land'** refers to everything permanently attached to the earth and the words **'beneficial enjoyment'** denotes convenience, advantage or any amenity or any necessity.

The owner or occupier referred to in the provision is known as the **Dominant Owner** and the land for the benefit of which the easementary right exists is called **Dominant Heritage**. Whereas the owner upon whose land the liability is imposed is known as the **Serviant Owner** and the land on which such a liability is imposed to do or prevent something, is known as the **Servient Heritage.**

Illustrations-

1. 'P' being the owner of certain land or house has a right of way over Q's house, adjacent to his house, to move out of the street. This is known as right of easement.

2. A voluntary dedication of right by 'X' to the public for passing or re-passing over a surface of certain land is not a right of easement.

3. X's right to go on his neighbour Y's household for fetching water from the well for the purpose of his own household is a right of easement. Here, the way to the well is through Y's land only. Hence, X has an easementary right to pass through Y's household.

According to Salmond, easement is that legal servient which can be exercised on some other piece of land specifically for the beneficial enjoyment of one's own land. Right of easement is basically a form of privilege, the integral part of which is to do an act or prevent certain acts on some other land for enjoyment of one's own land.

Other examples of right of easement includes-

- Right of way
- Right to discharge rainwater
- Right to sunlight etc

Essentials of Easements
1. Dominant and Servient Heritage
For the enjoyment of right of easement, necessary existence of two properties i.e dominant and servient heritage is a must. This is because as per the definition, it is the right exercised by the owner or occupier of one land for enjoying the benefit of his/her land, over the land of some other person. Dominant and servient heritage cannot be one. Thus, the existence of two properties and that to be separate from each other is essential.

2. Separate owners
For exercising the right of easements, owners of the two properties shall be different and not a single person.

3. Beneficial Enjoyment
The object of easements is that the dominant owner enjoys it in a way which includes express and implied benefits.

4. Positive or Negative
Easements can be both positive or negative. Former refers to a right through which the dominant owner does some act to exercise the right over the land of the servient owner. Whereas, the latter denotes an act of prevention. In a negative easement the dominant owner prevents or restricts the servient owner from doing certain act or acts.

In a right of easement an owner of dominant heritage can do an act or prevent the servient owner from doing something but he cannot bind the servient owner to do something for him.

The easementary right exists only when two heritages are adjacent to each other. It is a right in rem, which means a right available against the whole world. Easement as a right is always annexed to the dominant tenement. It is a right of re-aliena which means a right over a servient tenement and no on one's own land.

Classification of Easements

Section 5 of the The Indian Easements Act, 1882 classifies the easements as follows–

· **Continuous or Discontinuous**

Continuous easements are the one whose enjoyment may be continued without the intervention of any human conduct or act of a man. There is no interference by a man and it adds special quality to the property.

While, on the other hand, right of easement for the enjoyment which an interference of a man is required is known as discontinuous. In this kind of easement, it is necessary that a human act is done on the servient heritage.

· **Apparent or Non- Apparent**

An apparent easement is one the existence of which can be seen through a permanent sign. It can be visible by a careful examination and on reasonable foresightedness. It is also known as express easement. An inspection is required to check the existence of a right. For example- There is a drain from A's land to B's land and from there it led to an open yard. This can be visible through a clear inspection and is an apparent easement.

Whereas, a non-apparent easement is just opposite of what apparent easement is. This kind of easement is not visible through an inspection. There is no permanent sign as such. The right is in use but is not visible and thus, is known as an invisible easement. For example, A's right annexed to A's land to prevent B from building on his own house.

Limitations or Conditions of Easements

An easementary right may be permanent or for a period of years or for a limited term. It can also be subjected to periodical interruption or may be exercisable at a particular place, between certain hours and for a certain or particular purpose. This right can also be granted on a condition that such a right shall become void or voidable on happening of some event or non performing of some act. These limitations or conditions which regard to the right of easement has been specified under Section 6 of the Act.

Restrictive Easements

Section 7 specifies that the easements are restrictive of certain rights which are as follows-

- Exclusive right to enjoy
- Right to advantages arising out of the situation
- Profit a Prendre

According to The Indian Easements Act, 1882, profit a prendre is a part of the definition of easements. An instance to explain the concept is, a right to take earth from the land of the other person for making an earthenware is a profit a prendre. This is basically a profit made out of the land of the other person. Other examples of profit a prendre-

- Right of fishery
- Right to take fruits of trees in the season

This is the right which is exercised on the land appurtenant to the dominant heritage. Hence, there shall be the existence of two heritages i.e. dominant and servient. The owner of the dominant heritage exercises this right on the property of the servient owner. Profit a prendre is a right to do something on the land of servient tenement for more beneficial enjoyment of the dominant heritage.

Modes of Acquisition of Easements

1. Express Grant

The easement can be acquired through express grant made by inserting the clause of granting such a right in the deed of sale, mortgage or through any other form of transfer. This involves expressing by the grantor of his clear intention. If the value of the immovable property is Rs.100 or above then it compulsory for it to be in writing and duly registered.

2. Implied Circumstances

Easementary right can be acquired in implied circumstances in the following ways-

- **Easement of Necessity**

Section 13 of the act deals with this. This consists of the circumstances where the owner or occupier cannot use his property without exercising the right of easement over the servient heritage. Thus, absolute necessity is the test and the convenience.

For example– X sells his land to Y for agricultural purpose. Here, Y cannot access his land without passing through Z's land (his neighbour). Thus, this is an easement of necessity.

- **Quasi Easements**

Easements are quasi as those are arising out of circumstances,i.e. When common properties are converted into tenements by way of sale, mortgage, partition or through any other form of transfer. In such a case, there is an implied grant of right of easement.

For example– P's right attached to Q's house to receive air and light through a window without any obstruction by his neighbour. This is a continuous.

- **Prescriptive Easements**

Section 15 provides for this type. Following are the requisites-

1. Right must be definite and certain,
2. Right must have been independently enjoyed without any agreement with the servient owner,
3. Must be enjoyed openly, peacefully and as of a right without any interruption for a continuous period of 20 years and in respect of any government land the period of non-interruption shall be 30 years.

- **Customary Easements**

An easement right can be acquired by virtue of a local custom. This is known as customary easements. Section 18 of the Act provides for it.

For example- people living in a particular city or town having a right to bury the dead in a particular area or riparian right to use water.

Extinction of Easements

Section 37 to 47 of the The Indian Easements Act, 1882, provides for the mode of extinction of easements.

- **Dissolution of Servient Owner's right**

In the situation where the grantor ceases to have any right in the servient tenement because of some reason, then the right of easements ceases to exist as well. This has been specified under Section 37 of the Act. For eg- X grants a piece of land to Y for a period of 20 years in the year 1970. In the year 1971, Y imposed an easement in favour of Z. In 1990 Y's interest came to an end. Thus, easementary right granted to Z ceases to end as well.

- **Expiry of time or happening of an event**

When an easement is acquired on certain conditions or for certain purpose or for certain period of time. On the fulfilment of such condition or purpose or expiry of the time, the right of easement extinguishes as well as in accordance with Section 6 of the Act.

- **Extinction by release**

Where in a situation the owner of the dominant heritage releases the right of easement to the servient owner, the right ceases to exist. Such a release can be both expressly or impliedly made. For eg- P has a right to discharge water through the eaves to Q's yard. P authorized Q to construct a building to such a height as not be able to discharge water. Q builds it and P's right comes to an end.

- **Termination of necessity**

When necessity terminates the easement of necessity terminates as well. For example- A grants a piece of land to B on which easement of necessity for B is the right of his way over A's land. Later on, B purchases a part of the A's land over which he may pass to reach his own land. Here, the necessity has ended and so does the easement.

- **Useless Easements**

When easement is of such a nature that is not useful or becomes incapable of being beneficial at any time or under any circumstances, then the right of easement ends.

- **Permanent change in the Dominant Heritage**

When the nature of the dominant heritage changes permanently with increase in burden on tenement, then the right of easement ceases to exist as the purpose of it was the beneficial enjoyment of the dominant heritage. For example- A's house is located such that he has a right of way by passing through B's house. Later, due to earthquake, B's house got cut off and thus, right of easement ends.

- **Extinction by destruction of either of heritages**

When either of heritages gets destroyed, the easement ends as it is essential for two properties to exist for exercising the right.

- **Unity by ownership**

By unity of ownership it is indicated that when one person becomes the owner of both the dominant and servient heritage then the right of easement terminates. For instance, A has right of easement over B's property. Later on, A purchases B's property and becomes the owner of B's property. In such a case, easement extinguishes.

Suspension of Easements

Section 49 of the Act provides that easement can be suspended under the following circumstances-

An easement is or can be suspended when the dominant owner becomes entitled to the possession of servient heritage for a limited interest. An example which can be stated here to explain the concept is that A has a right of easement over B's land. In future A takes B's land on rent, here A becomes the occupier of B's land. Thus, easement suspends.

When the servient owner becomes entitled to the possession of dominant heritage for a limited interest, the easement is suspended.

Thus, where both the dominant and servient owner becomes one, easement is suspended.

Revival of Easements

Section 51 of the Act provides for the situations wherein easement suspended or extinguished can be revived, which are as follows-

When an easement is extinguished by destruction of either of the heritages then it can be revived-

If the heritage is restored in 20 years.

If the heritage is rebuilt in 20 years

2. In case of unity of ownership, if the unity breaks due to some reason, then easementary right can be revived and also through an order of a competent court.

Licenses

Section 52 of the Act deals with the concept of licenses. Where one person grants to another person a right to do or continue to do something in or upon the immovable property of the grantor, something which if he does will be unlawful without the prior permission or the availability of the grant. Such a right shall not amount to an easmentary right or creation of interest in the property.

Essentials of licenses

1. It is a permission granted, i.e a right arising out of permission.
2. Legalises an act.
3. Is revocable on the act of the grantor.
4. It is always in respect of immovable property.
5. It is a right in personam.

Revocation of licenses

License can be revoked in following ways-

If from the cause of preceding the grant, the grantor himself ceases to have any interest in the property, the license gets revoked. Grantor's interest comes to an end.

- **By express and implied release of the license by licensee.**

There are certain cases wherein a license is issued under certain conditions or limitations. This includes a license issued on a condition that if a certain act is doe or is not performed then the license may become void. In such a situation wherein these acts are performed then license can be revoked. Also, licenses are granted for the fulfillment of certain acts and once it is fulfilled license can be revoked.

Where a property in relation to which a license was granted gets destroyed due to any reason, then a license can be revoked.

Where, a licensee himself becomes the owner of the property for which license was granted, then the purpose for which license was granted ceases to exist and thus, the license also ceases to exist and gets terminated.

When licensee does not use it for a period of 20 years then the license gets revoked.

Transferable Licenses

According to **Section 56** of the Act, a license can be transferable under the following conditions-

A license to attend a place of public entertainment may be transferred by the licensee. This may be gathered from the grant or contract, or from surrounding circumstances or local usage.

For instance, P grants Q, a right to walk over P's field whenever he pleases. The right is not annexed to any immovable property of Q. The right cannot be transferred.

Transfer by licensee- The general rule is that the licensee cannot transfer his license. If he transfers then the transferee becomes a trespasser and can be or may be ejected.

Irrevocable Licenses

Section 60 provides that license can also be irrevocable. If the license is coupled with a transfer of property and the transfer is in force, it cannot be revoked. This is subject to the agreement. Hence, the power can be reserved. The rule is that a bare license may be revoked but if coupled with a transfer of the property, then it is irrevocable.

A license coupled with an interest in a land is binding. A license coupled with profit a prendre is irrevocable, for example, Right to excavate earth and carry it to make earthen wares, right to cut and carry timber on payment of royalty.

If the licensee, has executed some work which is permanent in nature and has incurred expenses, the licence cannot be revoked and hence, is irrevocable.

For example, there are two companies, namely X and Y having lands adjoining to each other. The agents were common who managed to put up the building and tank on X's land for use by Y.

License is irrevocable as the rule applied as was held in **Ramson V dyson.**